An Introduction to Machine Cutwork

by
Michelle Pullen

Acknowledgment And Thank You

To Vincent Matthews, my partner in business and life, your belief in me makes anything possible.

To my sister Susan Pullen for your devoted hours in helping with the diagrams.

To Margaret Smith who constructed all the garments so beautifully.

To Michelle Marvig for your talent in design and construction of the Mock Orange quilt.

To Bill and Margaret Blacka for opening up your home "Kanoona" for photography.

To Paul McIver for your energies and skill in photography.

To my favourite Mother in law Frances Matthews for your editing skills.

To Silkroad Australia for the hand painted silk used in the quilt.

To Veritage Press for their help and guidance.

To my Mum, for surrounding my childhood with fabrics and laces and passing on your creative genes.

Second edition

Author Michelle Pullen

ISBN 0 646 31567 6

Printed in Australia by: Veritage Press N.S.W

Published by: M.V.Designs, Australia, Michelle Pullen.

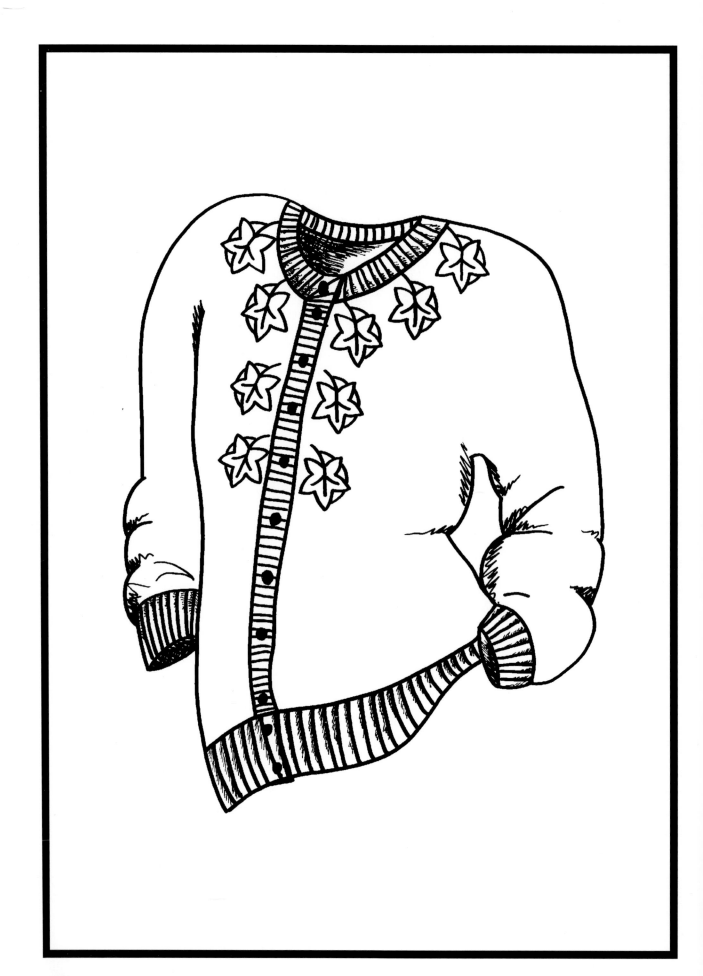

Foreword

Having been raised in a world full of fabrics, lace and notions, it is only natural that my art should be drawn towards creative sewing.

I have always admired the elegant beauty of hand stitched cutwork, but like many of us, do not have the time required to stitch by hand.

In the past machine cutwork was achieved by sewing a satin stitch and than cutting out the cutwork areas. I always felt this method unsatisfactory as it left frayed fabrics, creating an untidy edge.

To achieve a totally professional finish I have developed an easy three step method which totally encases the cutwork edge with stitching, leaving not a frayed edge in sight. Utilising a standard straight stitch and zig-zag and without using a hoop, you will find this technique achievable and rewarding for the beginner and inspiring to the advanced sewer.

I have designed the book as a sequence of lessons, starting with learning a satin stitch and taking you through basic to more advanced cutwork methods, the seven designs enclosed are made up of 32 sections, the sections can be joined together to create endless variations in style and shape, allowing you to add your own creative touch.

I trust you will enjoy stitching cutwork and hope your creations are held in loving hands by generations to come.

Yours sincerely

Michelle Pullen

Contents

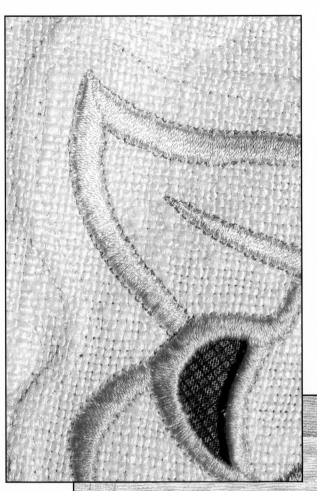

DESCRIPTION:
Cutwork Quilts? Why Not!!
Rich coloured threads stitched
onto silk add a unique embellishment to a treasured Heirloom.
(Photo also on back cover)

DESIGN:
Mock Orange

SECTION:
A + B

TECHNIQUES:
Multi coloured stitching, page 55
Outline Stitch, page 35
Mitered Point, page 32
Variable width Satin Stitch,
page 34

DESCRIPTION:
Strong bold colours and high fashion take Cutwork beyond the traditional and into the modern day.

DESIGN:
Lyrebird

SECTION:
A

TECHNIQUES:
Insertion - chiffon, page 57
Contrast colour, outline, page 35

DESCRIPTION:
Stitching a Cutwork Doily is a great beginners project and will add charm to your home decor.

DESIGN:
Alpine Flower

SECTION:
A + D

TECHNIQUES:
Edge Cutwork, page 46
Mitered point, page 32
Mitered point on a Cutwork
Edge, page 48

Your Sewing Machine

Sewing Machine

To create cutwork you will only require a basic straight stitch, zig-zag sewing machine. If your machine offers you a range of decorative stitches you can utilise these for adding decorative finishes, but they are not required for cutwork in general.

Care Of Your Machine

Keeping your machine in top condition means it will always be working at it's best. Refer to your sewing machine's manual for general maintenance instructions. If you regularly clean, oil and service your sewing machine, your time and money will be rewarded with trouble free sewing.

The Needle

Embroidery/Metafil needles; These needles are specialised and are designed for when you use a 30 weight or metallic thread. They are generally available in sizes 75/11 or 80/12 and have a universal point. Embroidery/Metafil needles have a larger eye than a standard needle, thus allowing the thicker threads to pass through the eye without breaking and splitting.

If you are stitching with a finer 40 weight thread, you can use a standard universal needle size 80/12 .

Pressure foot

You will require an open toe embroidery foot. If you do not already have one of these pressure feet they are available from sewing machine outlets for all makes and models of machines. Do not confuse this foot with the open darning foot. Refer to the diagram below. Fig 7A.

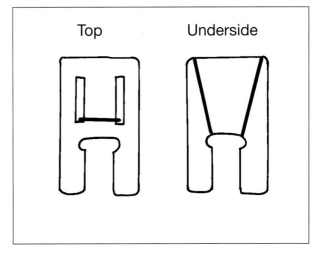

Fig 7A.

The open toe embroidery foot has a wide groove on the underside which allows the satin stitch to feed freely through the machine. It also allows maximum visibility of the stitch which is very important in achieving the best result.

Thread

Use the same thread top and bobbin.

Thread is a major component in the creation of cutwork. The finished look of your work will depend a great deal on the type of thread you use. Stitching cutwork with a standard thread is a no-no. Standard thread is dull and uneven, resulting in a dull uneven stitch. Where as machine embroidery threads have a sheen and are ultra smooth, resulting in a smooth, shiny, attractive stitch.

One important factor with cutworking is to use the same thread on the top and on the bobbin. Because of the nature of cutwork, you look through it, so at times the underside will be visible from the right side of the work.

There are three main types of machine embroidery threads available. Which one you decide to use will depend on the finish you wish to achieve. Whichever type of thread you choose, selecting a good reputable brand will save you the possible problems of breakage and knots. Listed below are the three main types of thread and their characteristics.

——————— *Types Of Thread* ———————

Rayon
Ultra shiny

Rayon machine embroidery thread is probably the most popular thread used for decorative sewing. Being spun from rayon / viscose it has a high sheen. It is available in different qualities. Keeping to a good brand will save frustration in dealing with knots and breakage.

Rayon thread can be stitched onto most fabrics, it is colour fast and fairly durable. If you are stitching onto 100% linen with rayon thread be careful when ironing. Long hot ironing may result in the thread being flattened due to melting. You can use rayon thread on 100% linen as long as you iron the article using lots of steam and sprayed water rather than hot, dry heat.

The two main weights available are, 30 heavy, 40 fine, both stitch well.

Cotton
Slight sheen

Cotton machine embroidery thread will give you a traditional finish as it imitates the cotton thread used for hand cutwork. Having less sheen than rayon embroidery thread it blends well on articles made from 100% linen or cotton. Cotton embroidery thread can also take the heat required to iron 100% linen fabric.

You will find a wide range of pastel shades available in cotton embroidery thread.

A good reputable brand will save the problems of knots and breakage. Also with poorer quality threads the darker colours may not be colour fast. If in doubt test sew and wash before starting your project.

The two main weights available are, 30 heavy, 40 fine, both stitch well.

Metallic
Glitzy

As the name implies this thread is made from metallic fibres. It is wonderful for that special occasion outfit such as the evening gown. As with all thread, quality is your guarantee against problems, so keep to a reputable brand.

If you have had problems stitching metallic thread in the past here are some problem solvers.

- Use a 40 weight or finer thread, these fine threads can also be used on the bobbin.

- Use an embroidery / Metafil needle.

The embroidery /Metafil needles have a larger eye than a standard needle, allowing the metallic thread to pass through the eye without splitting and breaking.

40 weight or finer for best result.

Fabric

Suitable Fabrics

Traditional hand cutwork is stitched onto medium weight woven fabric such as linen and cotton. These types of fabrics are also ideally suited to machine cutwork. Because of their ease of handling, I recommend them for that first time project. Linen look fabrics are also suitable, these fabrics are often made of man made fibres or a mixture of man made and natural fibres. You will generally find fabrics with a percentage of man made fibres crease resistant and less expensive than 100% linen.

We are not restricted to just the traditional types of fabrics for machine cutwork. Any medium to heavy weight woven fabric with a fairly tight weave may be used. We can also use medium/light to medium/heavy weight tightly knitted fabrics. The tightness of the weave and knit is important as the cutwork area is stitched three times. If the fabric is to loosely woven or knitted this amount of stitching will perforate the fabric, and the fabric will tear away from the stitching. If in doubt about using a fabric for machine cutwork, test sewing will determine whether it is suitable or not. All fabrics should be pre - washed to guard against shrinkage.

You may also stitch your cutwork onto ready made articles, knitwear is ideal for doing this.

Insertion Fabrics

Lace, organza, chiffon and cotton netting are all ideal to use as insertion fabrics. You will find detailed instructions on inserting such fabrics behind your cutwork areas on page 57.

▼▼▼▼▼▼▼▼▼▼▼▼▼▼▼▼▼▼▼▼▼▼▼▼▼▼▼▼▼▼▼▼▼▼

Embroidery Scissors

When cutting out the cutwork areas a good pair of embroidery scissors will make the job easier and neater. The investment in a good quality pair of scissors is well worth the money, just keep them hidden from husbands and children. Quality scissors will last most sewers a lifetime and will serve many a purpose besides cutwork.

Test cut before you buy, here is a list of features to look for when purchasing.

Scissor Check List

- How comfortable are the scissors in your hand? If you have large fingers you will be wanting a pair that will not cut off your blood circulation.

- Compare the quality of the steel, good quality steel will sharpen better and last longer.

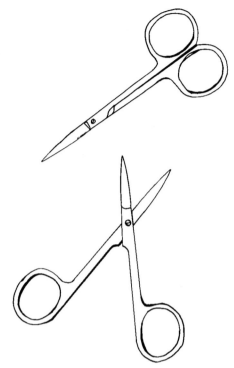

- How are the blades held together? This is very important, a scissor which is held together with a screw means the blade tension can be re tightened after sharpening. If the blades are riveted together the scissors will be useless after sharpening as the blade tension will be loose and the rivets cannot to be tightened.

- How fine is the point? Do they cut all the way to the point?

- You will find there are straight and curved bladed scissors available. I find the curved blade particularly good for cutwork as the curve allows you to cut very close to the stitching. This is handy when trimming in Step Two of the cutwork stages.

Fig 10A.

▼▼▼▼▼▼▼▼▼▼▼▼▼▼▼▼▼▼▼▼▼▼▼▼▼▼▼▼▼▼▼

Fabric Stabilisers

Stabilising of the fabric is very important. Stabilising will not only prevent the fabrics from stretching and puckering, it will also give you a better stitch quality.

In the past tissue paper was used to stabilise fabrics for embroidering. Tissue paper worked well when stitching on the straight grain of the fabric, yet the fabric still stretched and puckered when stitching on the cross grain / bias or when stitching on knitted fabric.

Thank heavens for the modern day! We now have specialised iron on papers and liquid stabilisers to overcome these problems.

Iron on papers

These papers are designed to iron onto the wrong side of the fabric behind the design area. Because they iron on, they will hold the knit or weave of the fabric firmly, preventing the fabric from stretching and puckering, even on the cross grain / bias.

Once stitching is completed they will tear away from the work without leaving any adhesive on the fabric. These papers are available in different weights. I have found the heavier paper causes the embroidery thread to split and break and will not come away from the stitching easily. The iron on paper I use is known as Fabric Stabiliser. Being light weight it causes no problems with the thread or removal.

Using Fabric Stabiliser

Fabric Stabiliser has one smooth shiny surface, this is the adhesive side. Cut a piece of stabiliser slightly larger than your chosen cutwork design. Place the shiny side of the Stabiliser onto the wrong side of your fabric covering the design area. Using an iron temperature to suit your fabric, press the stabiliser onto your fabric.

Applying pressure to the iron will iron the stabiliser on firmly. How much pressure you use will vary from fabric to fabric, test on a scrap of fabric first. You want the stabiliser to adhere well and tear off the fabric easily. You may find that due to handling the Fabric Stabiliser will lift off some fabrics during the course of sewing. If this occurs simply re-iron it down through out the stitching process.

If working on fleecy backed fabrics, test to check that when the stabiliser is torn off it does not remove the fleece with it. This can happen, especially with economically priced fabrics. If there is a problem with the fleece being removed, simply iron the stabiliser on very lightly using a cool iron (permanent press).

Recycling Tip

Fabric Stabiliser is re-useable. You will notice when the Fabric Stabiliser is removed no adhesive remains on the fabric, the adhesive always stays on the Fabric Stabiliser. This allows you to re-iron the stabiliser onto your next project. I keep a scrap bag of stabiliser for re-use, all the good size pieces go into my bag and I use them for future projects. It's not a problem if I need to overlap the pieces to cover an area as it still works just fine.

Liquid Stabiliser

Liquid stabiliser, as the name implies, is designed to be applied to the fabric wet. It is then allowed to dry, this stiffens the fabric and creates a stable surface to stitch onto. Liquid stabiliser can be used in place of Fabric Stabiliser or in conjunction with Fabric Stabiliser. I find it useful when stitching onto fabrics such as voile because it gives extra support to softer fabrics. Once stitching is complete, wash the article in water to remove the liquid stabiliser.

Magic Fabric / Solvi

Magic Fabric, (also known as Solvi) is a water soluble fabric. It is used not so much to stabilise the fabric but to stabilise the cutwork edge in Step Three of the cutwork process. When stitching in Step Three of the cutwork process a satin stitch is sewn over the edge of the fabric (For detailed instructions on the three steps of cutwork refer to chapter 3). Now we all know what it's like to try and stitch right on the edge of a piece of fabric. The machine and the sewer have problems with the fabric feeding through the machine evenly. This is caused by the fabric not covering the feed dogs completely. To avoid this from happening when stitching a cutwork edge, the Magic Fabric is pinned behind the design area in Step Three of the cutwork process. This supplies a complete surface over the feed dogs, eliminating any problems with handling. Once the stitching is complete the Magic Fabric just washes out in luke warm water, leaving no residue even under the stitching. Another wonder of the modern day!

TIP: Magic Fabric is sensitive to moisture in the air. To prevent it from becoming soft and limp keep it stored in a closed plastic bag. Giving it a quick iron with a dry iron and a press cloth will remove any moisture from it.

Other Supplies

Vanish- A-Way

Vanish-A-Way was known as Vanishing Muslin in the 60's and 70's. It is a very firm fabric which can be stitched onto and will turn to a powder when ironed, vanishing. It is used in the creation of intricate Richelieu bars, I will be referring to Vanish-A-Way on page 59 "Richelieu Bars".

Marking pens and pencils

You will need a means of transferring the design onto the fabric. Detailed instructions on transferring the designs can be found on page 67.

Water Erasable Marking Pens

These pens are ideal to use as the marks will wash out in water. Used in conjunction with a light box they are excellent as a means of transferring the design.

Transfer Pencils

These pencils are generally available in pink or green. When using these pencils to transfer a design, the design is traced onto paper, the tracing you have made becomes a transfer which is then ironed onto the fabric. The marks on most fabrics, will be permanent, this means you need to ensure the stitching covers the transfer lines.

Dressmaker Carbon Paper

You will need dressmaker carbon paper to transfer your design if working on a dark coloured fabric. For some extra tips on making the lines clearly visible refer to page 67.

Light Box

Light boxes give a source of light underneath your fabric and design, making the design clearly visible for tracing. You can make a temporary light box following the instructions on page 68. If you invest in a professional light box I'm sure you will wonder how you ever lived without it.

Care Of Your Finished Cutwork

Laundering

How your article is laundered will depend mainly upon your chosen fabric. When purchasing fabric read the laundering instructions on the bolt of fabric. If like most of us you are a collector of fabric (notice I didn't say hoarder) it's a good idea to have the store staple a little note with the laundering instructions on it to your purchase. You will thank yourself in the future for the little trouble it takes to do this. Do dry clean your article if this is what the fabric requires. I try to avoid fabrics which require dry cleaning if my article is something which will require regular laundering, such as a blouse.

Fabrics which are washable are best washed by hand and hung to drip dry. You will find cutwork quite durable and long lasting. I have blouses that have been washed and washed by hand and they still look like new.

Pressing

The iron temperature should be set to suit the type of fabric. Lay two or three towels down on your ironing board to create padding which will prevent the embroidery from being flattened. Iron from the wrong side. One thing to be careful of when ironing is that the point of the iron does not get caught in the cutwork areas, this can cause the iron to pull and tear the fabric. For safety, iron using a pressing cloth to protect your work.

If you are ironing 100% linen and have stitched with rayon embroidery thread, be aware that long hot ironing may result in the thread being flattened due to slight melting. This will only occur with extreme heat. You can use rayon thread on 100% linen without problems as long as the article is ironed using steam and sprayed water to eliminate the creases from the fabric rather than a hot dry heat.

Satin Stitch

A satin stitch is a zig-zag with the stitch length decreased to form a close dense stitch and is the primary stitch used in the finish of cutwork. It's easy to learn how to satin stitch professionally and once learnt not easily forgotten.

You may wish to stitch the practice sheet at the end of this chapter. It is designed to teach you the principles of satin stitching and allow you to have a play, so you can fully enjoy the pleasures of sewing this beautiful stitch.

A Few Tips To Start With

- Your sewing machine manual should have a section on satin stitching, it's worth while reading this section as it will have been written for your machine. The settings quoted in your manual will be average settings, keep in mind they will differ slightly with fabric weights and thread thicknesses.

- Use good quality machine embroidery thread on the top and bobbin of your machine.

- Fit your sewing machine with an open toe embroidery pressure foot.

- Test sewing is important to ensure your machine settings are correct before you start your project. To test sew :

    * Stabilise a scrap of fabric from your project.

    * Thread your machine top and bobbin with the thread you intend to use.

    * Sew, make any adjustments required and sew again until you are happy with the stitch.

- If you are unsure of the appropriate tension setting for your machine, test sew using a contrasting coloured thread on your bobbin. This will enable you to see clearly how the stitch reacts as you adjust the tension setting.

- One of the main mistakes made when satin stitching is having the stitch length too close. If you feel you have to pull or drag on the fabric and the stitch is bunching up, you need to increase the stitch length. It is better to have the stitch slightly open than too close which will cause the above problems.

- Take the time to play, this is often where the most is learnt and confidence is built. The practice sheet at the end of this chapter has been designed for just that.

DESCRIPTION:
The simple beauty of the Rock Rose design adds an elegant country look to this dress.

DESIGN:
Rock Rose

SECTION:
A

TECHNIQUES:
Insertion as a lining, page 57
Outline stitch, page 35
Tapered point, page 33

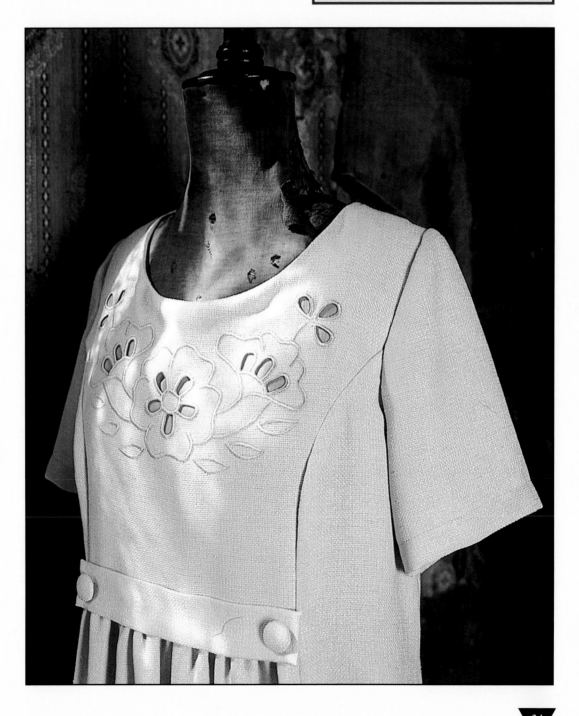

DESCRIPTION:
Sewn using a Satin and Blanket Stitch in Multi-colours, creates a charming country look to this Doona cover.

DESIGN:
Rock Rose

SECTION:
A.B.C.

TECHNIQUES:
Multi-coloured stitching, page 55
Blanket stitch, page 37
Outline stitch, page 35
Combining Design sections, page 75

DESCRIPTION:

Table linen will always hold its place through the ages. The Ivy cloth displays combining a single design section to create a larger scale design. The versatility of the designs allow you to add your own creativeness,

DESIGN:

Ivy

SECTION:

B

TECHNIQUES:

Combining Design Sections, page 74
Single contrast colour Stitching, page 55

Machine Settings

Stitch width

The width of the stitch can vary depending on your personal preference and the type of fabric you are stitching. A wider stitch will give a bolder finish and is suited to larger designs. A narrower stitch will give a finer finish and is suited to smaller designs.

It is important when satin stitching on a cutwork edge that the stitch width does not go below 2.3mm. Too narrow a stitch on the cutwork edge can result in the fabric pulling out from under the stitch. The cutwork edge needs at least this width to give it strength and durability for washing and wearing.

If your sewing machines stitch width adjustments are made by increment ie: increased by 0.5mm at a time, you may find that when stitching a variable width satin stitch the edge of the stitch is uneven. If this happens it can be corrected by outlining the satin stitch with either a straight stitch or zig-zag, refer to page 35.

Stitch Length

The stitch length on an average, is set between 0.6mm and 0.4mm. The exact setting will vary from machine to machine and will also be influenced by thread thickness. Test sewing is important to determine the correct setting for your project. A common mistake made with satin stitching is having the stitch length to close. This will result in the stitch bunching up, particularly on corners and curves. The stitch should flow through the machine without you having to drag or pull on the fabric.

Thread Tension

To achieve a smooth, neat finish to your satin stitch, the thread tension is adjusted so that the top thread is pulled to the underside of the stitch. To help you to understand this, thread your machine with a different coloured thread on the bobbin to what you have on the top. How the stitch reacts as you adjust the tension will then be clearly visible. Remember test sewing is the key to achieving a perfect stitch. Following is a guide for thread tension adjustment for different machines.

Computerised Machines

Some computerised machines really do have automatic tension, meaning the machine will literally move the tension dial for you when you select satin stitch. In some cases due to thread thickness computerised machines will need the tension dial adjusted further, manually. If you are adjusting the tension manually, you will be taking the tension dial to a smaller number. Test sewing will tell you if you need to adjust the tension further than the machine has done automatically, and by how much.

Threading The Bobbin Case

The following information refers to Husquvarna models 1250, 1200 and 1070 as well as all Bernina machines except model 1630. The bobbin cases on these machines have a hole in the finger which is designed to be threaded when satin stitching. By threading the bobbin case you will be tightening the bobbin tension, which will result in the top thread being pulled to the underside of the stitch. If after threading the bobbin case and test sewing, you find the tension needs further adjustment, you will need to adjust the top tension dial as well as having the bobbin case threaded. To adjust the top tension dial, take it to a smaller number or with some models, in the direction of the "minus" symbol. To what degree you adjust the top tension dial if required, will vary from machine to machine as well as with thread thickness.

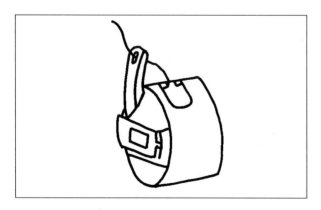

Fig 16A.

Other Sewing Machines

To achieve the optimum stitch the top tension dial will need to be taken to a smaller number, thus loosening the top thread tension. How much you decrease the top tension dial will vary from machine to machine. There will also be variations due to thread thickness. I have stitched on machines where the tension has been taken all the way to 0 and on other machines where the tension is only slightly adjusted. Test sew to determine the correct tension setting for your machine.

How The Stitch Should Look

The stitch should be even and flat with no

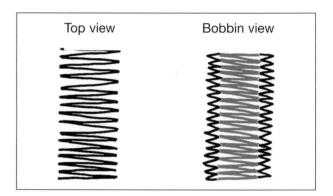

Fig 16B.

bobbin thread showing from the top of the stitch. Fig 16B.

- If the bobbin thread is showing on the top of the stitching you need to loosen the top thread tension.

- If the top thread is looping, the top thread tension is too loose, you will need to tighten it.

Tying Off The Threads

We need to ensure the threads are secured at the beginning and the end of each row of stitching to prevent them from unravelling. Fortunately we don't have to hand tie every thread, the following tricks will save you a lot of time as well as giving your work a professional and durable finish.

Over - Sewing

Method 1: If a row of stitching is to be sewn over by another row of stitching there is no need to tie the threads off. The oversewing will secure the stitching under it. This will often happen automatically as you stitch the design, but keep in mind to ensure the under stitching is placed appropriately so the oversewing will catch it. Fig 21A.

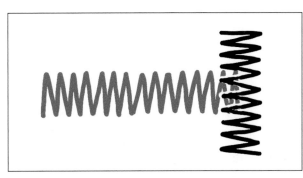

Fig 21A.

Method 2: When starting a row of stitching which will not be oversewn by method one, the following trick will allow you to oversew, eliminating the need to tie off the threads.

1. With your machine set on satin stitch, set the stitch width to 0.

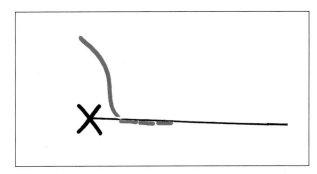

Fig 21B.

2. Position your work so you will be stitching approximately 0.5 cm forward from the start of the row of stitching.

3. Sew 3 to 5 stitches. Fig 21B.

4. Leave the needle down in the fabric.

5. Using your embroidery scissors, cut the top tail thread. There is no need to trim the bobbin thread as it can be trimmed once the row of stitching is complete. Fig 21C.

Fig 21C.

6. Raise the needle and the pressure foot and drag the stitching so you are in position at the beginning of the row to be sewn.

7. Increase the stitch width and complete the row of stitching, you will be oversewing the first stitches you sewed, securing them perfectly. Fig 22A.

Fig 22A.

Tying Off The Threads By Hand

By using the above oversewing methods you will eliminate the need to tie off by hand quite a lot. You will still need to tie off manually when a row cannot be oversewn. To tie off by hand professionally:

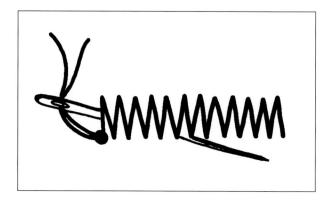

Fig 22B.

1. Pull the top thread to the back of your work.

2. Tie a knot.

3. Thread the two threads onto a fine hand sewing needle and run the tail threads under the satin stitch. Fig 22B.

4. Trim the excess thread.

Stitch Techniques

Satin Stitching Curves

To achieve smooth flowing curves and round shapes we will use a method known as pivoting. Pivoting refers to the technique of leaving the needle down in the fabric and turning the work. It is mainly tight curves that require pivoting, long slight curves can generally be stitched in a continuous row of sewing. You will know when a curve needs pivoting as you will see the stitch going out of alignment to the design line.

A very tight curve will require pivoting every 3 to 5 stitches. The more open a curve the less pivoting required. Fig 23A.

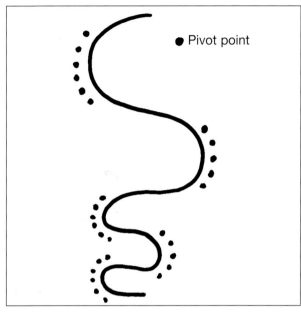

Fig 23A.

To Pivot

1. Leave the needle down in the fabric on the outside edge of the curve. Fig 23B.

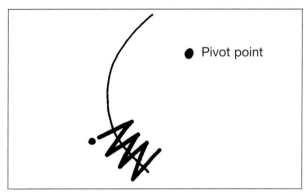

Fig 23B.

2. Raise the pressure foot.

3. Pivot the fabric slightly.

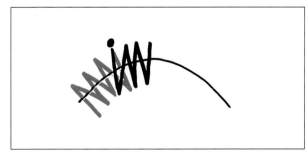

Fig 23C.

4. Lower the pressure foot and continue stitching, the next stitch should slightly overlap the previous stitch. Fig 23C.

Opp's, It Doesn't Look Right

If your curves have gaps in the stitching you are leaving the needle on the inside of the curve instead of the outside of the curve. Fig 24A.

If your curves have sharp angles to them you are not pivoting enough and pivoting too sharply. Fig 24B.

Fig 24A.   Fig 24B.

Satin Stitching Right Angle Corners

There are two choices on how to stitch a right angle corner. Which one you decide to use is your own personal preference. If your sewing machines stitch width adjustments are made by increments ie: increased by 0.5mm at a time you will not be able to achieve an even flow to a mitred corner, in which case it will be better for you to stitch the standard right angle corner.

Standard Corner

1. Stitch 3 to 5 stitches past the corner.

2. Leave the needle down in the fabric on the same side of the stitching as the direction you are turning.

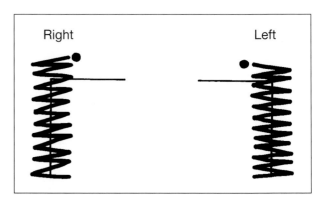

Fig 24C.

Left hand turn: When turning left, the needle is down in the fabric on the left hand side of the stitch. Fig 24C.

Right hand turn: When turning right, the needle is left down in the fabric on the right hand side of the stitch. Fig 24C.

3. Raise the pressure foot and pivot in the direction of the next row of stitching.

4. Raise the needle and realign the fabric so the needle goes into the point it last came out of. Lower the pressure foot and continue sewing. Fig 25A.

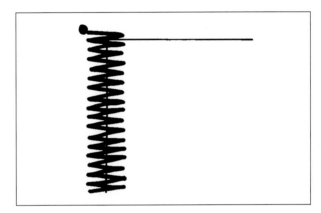

Fig 25A.

Mitred Corner

If your sewing machines stitch width adjustments are made by increments ie: increased by 0.5mm at a time you may not be able to achieve an even flow to a mitred corner. If this happens it can be corrected by outlining the stitch, refer to page 35.

1. Stitch to the corner, leaving the needle down in the fabric on the outside point of the corner. Fig 25B.

2. Raise the pressure foot and pivot.

3. Decrease the stitch width to 0.5mm

4. Raise the needle and realign so the needle goes into the point it last came out off. Lower the pressure foot.

5. With your hand on the stitch width dial start stitching, increasing the width as you sew. Fig 25C.

Note: Stitch slowly yet increase the stitch width rapidly, you want the last stitch that oversews the first row of sewing to be of equal width as that of the first row.

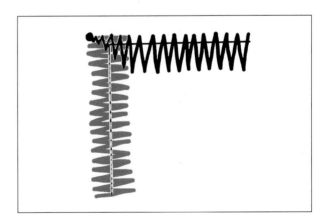
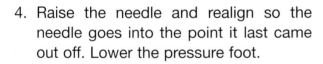

Fig 25B.

Fig 25C.

Satin Stitching Points

We have three choices in how to stitch a point. If your sewing machines stitch width adjustments are made by increments ie: increased by 0.5mm at a time you may not be able to achieve an even flow to a mitred point or a tapered point. If this happens it can be corrected by outlining the stitch, refer to page 35.

Standard Point

A standard point is stitched completely with the same stitch width.

1. Stitch all the way to the end of the point.

2. Leave the needle down in the fabric at the outside edge of the point. Fig 26A.

3. Raise the pressure foot and pivot the fabric so you are aligned to stitch the next row. Lower the pressure foot.

4. Raise the needle and realign the fabric so the needle goes into the point it last came out of. Lower the pressure foot and continue sewing. You will be stitching over the first row of sewing. Fig 26B.

Mitred Point

If your sewing machines stitch width adjustments are made by increments ie: increased by 0.5mm at a time you may not be able to achieve an even flow to a mitred point. If this happens it can be corrected by outlining the stitch, refer to page 35.

1. Stitch all the way to the end of the point, keeping the angle of the stitch in line with the point. Leave the needle down in the fabric on the outside edge of the point. Fig 26C.

2. Raise the pressure foot and pivot.

3. Decrease the stitch width to 0.5mm

4. Raise the needle and realign so the needle goes into the point it last came out of. Lower the pressure foot.

5. With your hand on the stitch width dial start stitching, increasing the width as you sew. Fig 26D.

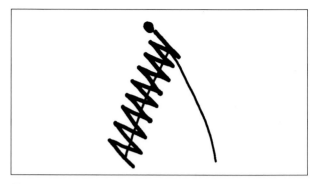

Fig 26A.

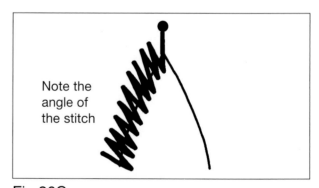

Fig 26B.

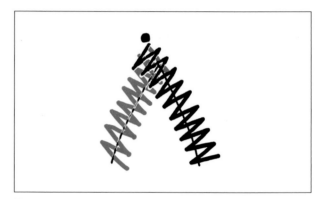

Note the angle of the stitch

Fig 26C.

Fig 26D.

Note: Stitch slowly yet increase the stitch width rapidly, you want the last stitch that oversews the first row of sewing to be of equal width as that of the first row.

Tapered Point

If your sewing machines stitch width adjustments are made by increments ie: increased by 0.5mm at a time you may not be able to achieve an even flow to a tapered point. If this happens it can be corrected by outling the stitch, refer to page 35.

1. As you stitch up to the point, decrease the stitch width down to 0. Fig 27A.

2. Leaving the needle down in the fabric, raise the pressure foot, pivot so you are aligned to stitch the next row. Lower the pressure foot.

3. Increase the width as you sew down the point. Fig 27B.

Tapered Point On A Cutwork Edge

If your sewing machines stitch width adjustments are made by increments ie: increased by 0.5mm at a time you may not be able to achieve an even flow to a tapered point. If this happens it can be corrected by outlining the stitch, refer to page 35.

Note: It is important when satin stitching on an edge that the stitch width does not go below 2.3mm. Too narrow a stitch on the cutwork edge can result in the fabric pulling out from under the stitch. The cutwork edge needs at least this width to give it strength and durability for washing and wearing. A tapered point is formed by decreasing the width of the stitch as the point is sewn. The secret in stitching a tapered point on a cutwork edge is to extend the point beyond the cutwork edge,

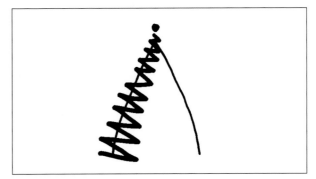

Fig 27A.

Fig 27B.

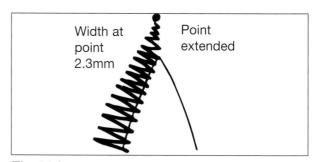

▼ Satin Stitch

1. As you stitch up to the point, decrease the stitch width. Keep to a width of at least 2.3mm on the cutwork edge, as the stitch goes beyond the cutwork edge decrease the width down to 0. Fig 28A.

2. Leaving the needle down in the fabric, raise the pressure foot, pivot so you are aligned to stitch the next row. Lower the pressure foot.

3. Increase the width as you sew down the point, again ensuring the width is at least set to 2.3mm by the time the stitching falls on the cutwork edge. Fig 28B.

Fig 28A.

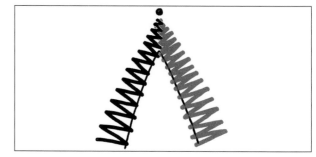

Fig 28B.

Variable Width Satin Stitch

Varying the width of the stitch while sewing truly brings a satin stitch to life by creating movement and dimension. A beautiful stitch to sew, it blends perfectly with mitred or tapered points. It is your decision when to vary the width and by how much, being the reason why this is one of my favourite stitches, as it allows room for self expression. Following are a few tips to help you sew this stitch to perfection.

•   If your sewing machines stitch width adjustments are made by increments ie: increased by 0.5mm at a time you may not be able to achieve an even flow to a variable satin stitch. If this happens it can be corrected by outlining the stitch, refer to page 35.

•   Adjust the width in accordance with the speed you are sewing. If you are sewing slowly the width will be adjusted at a slower speed than if you were sewing fast.

•   A gradual increase and decrease in width will look better than a sudden change in width.

•   When stitching on a cutwork edge do not go any narrower than 2.3mm. To narrow a stitch on the cutwork edge can result in the fabric pulling out from under the stitch. The cutwork edge needs at least this width to give it strength and durability against washing and wearing.

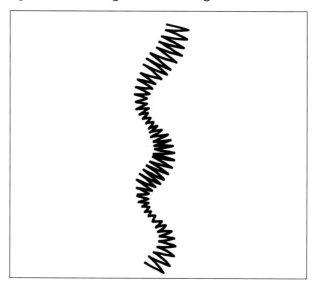

Fig 28C.

Outline Stitches

Adding That Extra Touch

It's amazing how the simplicity of these stitches can add such a wonderful finish to your satin stitching. Try them and I'm sure you will find it hard not to include them in your projects.

An uneven edge on a satin stitch can occur on fabrics that have a slub, by outlining the satin stitch with a straight stitch or open zig - zag you can actually neaten the edge.

Straight Stitch

Outlining a satin stitch with a straight stitch will add a slight padded look to the stitch. You can use the same coloured thread as the satin stitch, or to highlight your stitch a contrasting coloured thread.

It is most often easiest to outline your cutwork once all the satin stitching is complete. By doing this you will reduce the need to tie off.

Machine Settings

    Straight stitch

    Stitch Width: 0

    Stitch length: 1.5

    Tension: normal

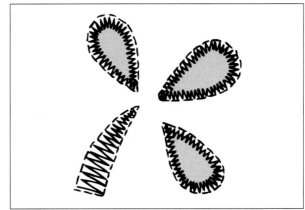

Fig 29A.

- A stitch length of 1.5 is used as it allows you to manoeuvre and pivot around corners and curves easily, giving a smooth flow to the stitch. Fig 29A.

- Stitch at a slow to medium speed, stitching right up against the satin stitch edge.

- Tie off the threads by taking them to the back off the work, tie a knot and run the tail threads under the satin stitch using a hand sewing needle. Fig 29B.

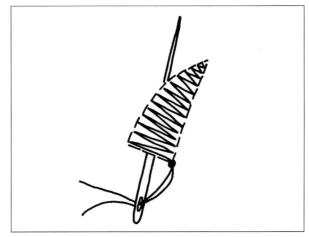

Fig 29B.

Outlining The Design With A Straight Stitch

You can also outline your design using a straight stitch. I do this when I feel the design needs something to tie it together or needs a little something extra to finish it off.

Machine Settings

Straight stitch

Stitch Width: 0

Stitch length: 1.5

Tension: normal

- A stitch length of 1.5 is used as it allows you to manoeuvre and pivot around corners and curves easily, giving a smooth flow to the stitch.

- Use the pressure foot as a guide for the stitch distance away from the satin stitch, 6mm. Fig 30A.

- If you like you can stitch more than one row of straight sewing as an outline.

- Tie off the threads by taking them to the back off the work, tie a knot and using a hand sewing needle weave the tail threads under the stitch. Fig 30B.

Fig 30A.

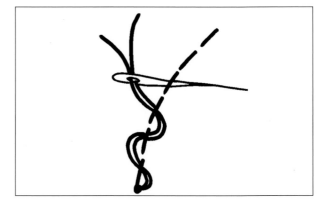

Fig 30B.

Zig - Zag

Outlining with a zig - zag adds something a little different and a richness to the satin stitch. It will also add a slight padded look to the stitch. You can use the same coloured thread as the satin stitch, or to highlight your stitch a contrasting coloured thread.

It is most often easiest to outline your cutwork once all the satin stitching is complete. By doing this you will reduce the need to tie off.

Machine Settings

Zig -zag

Stitch width: 1.5

Stitch length: 1.5

Tension: normal

- You can increase the width setting by up to 1mm if you like for a slightly bolder look.

- Stitch at a slow to medium speed, stitching right up against the satin stitch edge. Fig 31A.

- Tie off the threads by taking them to the back off the work, tie a knot and run the tail threads under the satin stitch using a hand sewing needle.

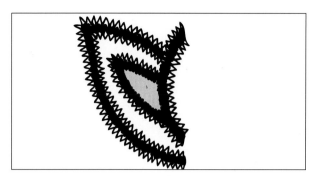

Fig 31A.

Blanket Stitch

By using the blind hem stitches on your machine you can interpret a hand sewing blanket stitch. The finished result giving a pleasant country look. There are two blindhem stitches which can be used to create a blanket stitch, which one you use will be determined by which stitch your machine offers you, if you have the choice of both all the better.

Blanket Stitch # One

This is what is known as a stretch blindhem stitch, a utility stitch designed for hemming stretch fabrics. By selecting this stitch and decreasing the stitch length you will achieve the look of a blanket stitch. The structure of this stitch creates a zig - zag with a blanket edge all in one motion. Fig 31B.

Fig 31B.

Machine Settings

    Stretch blindhem
    Stitch width: 6mm
    Stitch length: 0.5mm
    Tension: as for satin stitch

- Stitch curves as you would stitch a satin stitch curve, pivoting when needed. Stitch corners and points using the standard satin stitch point and corner method. Your corners and points will look extra nice if you allow one blanket stitch to be sewn at the very point. Fig 31C.

- Tie off the threads by taking them to the back off the work, tie a knot and run the tail threads under the stitch using a hand sewing needle. Fig 31D.

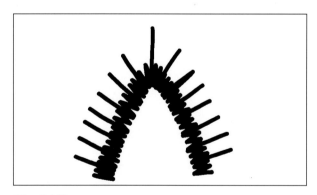

Fig 31C.

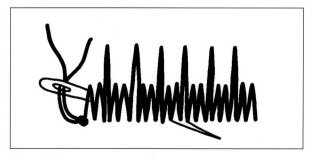

Fig 31D.

Blanket Stitch # 2

This stitch is created by using a woven blindhem stitch and a satin stitch. The woven blindhem stitch is a utility stitch designed for hemming woven fabrics. By selecting this stitch and decreasing the stitch length you will achieve the look of a blanket stitch. Because it forms a straight stitch on one edge this edge needs to be stitched over with a satin stitch. Fig 32A.

It is best to complete each row of stitching of your design with the two stitches before stitching the next area.

Machine Settings

One

Woven blindhem

Stitch width: 4mm

Stitch length: 3mm

Tension: normal

- Stitch the blindhem stitch so the straight edge falls on the design lines. Fig 32B

- Stitch curves as you would stitch a satin stitch curve, pivoting when needed. Your corners and points will look extra nice if you allow one blanket stitch to be sewn at the very point.

- There is no need to tie off the threads as they will be oversewn by the satin stitch.

Two

Zig - Zag

Stitch width: 3mm or variable

Stitch length: 0.5

Tension: as for satin stitch

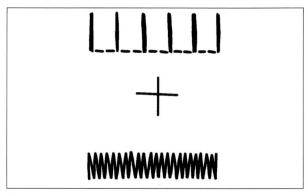

Fig 32A.

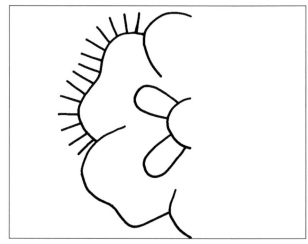

Fig 32B.

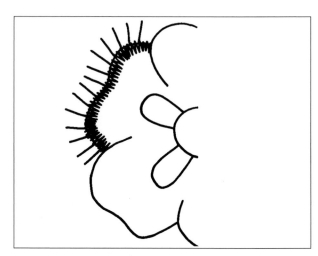

Fig 32C.

- You can satin stitch using the one set width or you may also use the variable width satin stitch.

- Satin stitch over the straight edge of the blindhem stitch. Fig 32C.

Practice Sheet

I have included the following practice sheet hoping to encourage you to take the time to play with the various satin stitch techniques. Stitching the practice sheet will allow you to get the feel for satin stitching. Not only will you use a satin stitch for cutwork it can also be used for applique and general machine embroidery, making a satin stitch well worth while perfecting as you will use this stitch often for decorative sewing.

Requirements

- Calico or like fabric (U.S.A. muslin).
- Fabric Stabiliser.
- Two contrast coloured machine embroidery threads.
- For 40 weight thread a universal 80/12 needle. For 30 weight thread a embroidery / metafil needle.
- Open toe embroidery pressure foot.
- Fabric marking pen.
- Fine point hand sewing needle.
- Scissors and pins.

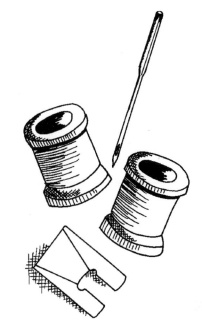

Symbols Used On The Practice Sheet

x-> Starting point and direction of sewing

● The point the needle is left in when pivoting (indication only)

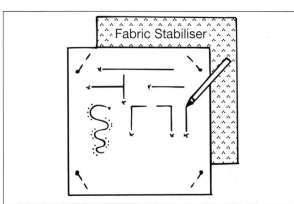

Fig 33B.

1. Photocopy the practice sheet first if you wish. Pin your fabric over the practice sheet and trace off the lines including the symbols.

2. Iron the Fabric Stabiliser to the wrong side of the fabric.

3. Fit your sewing machine with thread, pressure foot and needle. Use a contrast colour thread on the bobbin so you can see what happens to the stitch as you adjust the tension.

4. Go to the beginning of this chapter and stitch the related areas, referring to the diagrams as you sew.

Relax and have fun.

Satin Stitch Practice Sheet

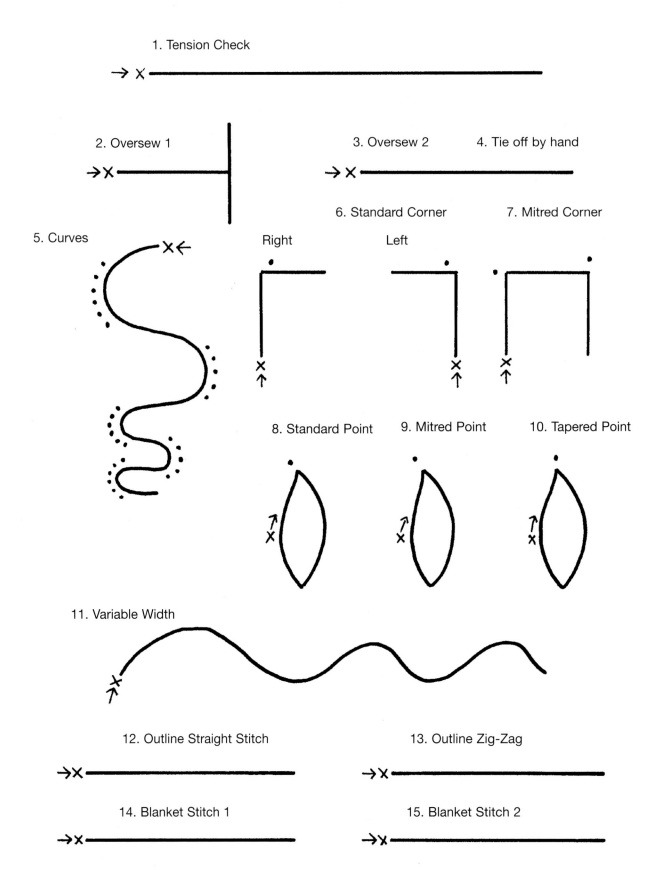

1. Tension Check

2. Oversew 1

3. Oversew 2   4. Tie off by hand

6. Standard Corner   7. Mitred Corner

5. Curves

Right   Left

8. Standard Point   9. Mitred Point   10. Tapered Point

11. Variable Width

12. Outline Straight Stitch   13. Outline Zig-Zag

14. Blanket Stitch 1   15. Blanket Stitch 2

The Three Steps Of Cutwork

In the past machine cutwork has been stitched by satin stitching and then cutting the fabric away from the cutwork areas. This of course left frayed fabric on the cutwork edge, resulting in an untidy finish. The technique we will be using first prepares the cutwork edge so we can satin stitch over it, encasing the edge completely with the satin stitch eliminating any frayed fabric from showing. This is a more professional and attractive finish than the old way as well as being stronger and more durable. The diagrams shown are the Ivy design, a great first time design to sew as it is quick and easy to stitch. The technique of course relates to any design you may choose to stitch. The machine settings relate to woven fabric, if stitching onto knitted fabric please refer to page 56 " Knitted Fabrics".

Preparation

- Fit your sewing machine with an open toe embroidery foot.

- Thread your machine top and bobbin with machine embroidery thread.

- If using 40 weight thread fit your machine with a universal 80/12 needle.

- If using 30 weight thread fit your machine with a embroidery / metafil needle.

- Transfer your chosen design to the right side of your fabric, marking the areas to be cut out.

- Iron the Fabric Stabiliser to the wrong side of your fabric, covering the design area.

Fig 35A.

Step One

Step one stay stitches the cutwork edge, adding strength and preventing the fabric from stretching, especially on the cross grain.

Machine Settings

Straight stitch

Stitch width: O

Stitch length 1.5

Tension: Normal

1. Straight stitch around all shapes to be cut out, reverse stitching at the beginning and end of each row of sewing, this row of stitching will be oversewn so there is no need to tie the threads off, they can simply be cut off. You are sewing around the cutwork areas only, not the whole design. Fig. 36A.

2. Using embroidery scissors cut out the inner fabric and fabric stabiliser from each cutwork area. To avoid cutting the stitching, cut 1mm away from the stitching. You don't have to cut absolutely exact as Step Two will neaten any imperfect cutting. Fig 36A.

Step Two

Step Two is designed to add strength to the cutwork edge as well as allowing you to trim any excess fraying fabric away from the edge before satin stitching.

Machine Settings

Zig - Zag

Stitch width: 1.5

Stitch Length: 0.8mm

Tension: Normal

1. Zig - Zag around all shapes that are cut out, centreing the zig - zag over the row of straight stitching. Reverse stitch at the beginning and end of each row of stitching. This row of stitching will be oversewn so there is no need to tie the threads off, they can simply be cut off. You are sewing around the cutwork areas only, not the whole design. Fig 36B

2. Using embroidery scissors, trim any fraying fabric away from the stitching. Fig 36C.

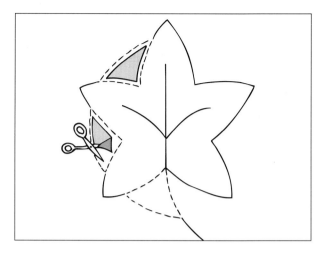

Fig 36A.

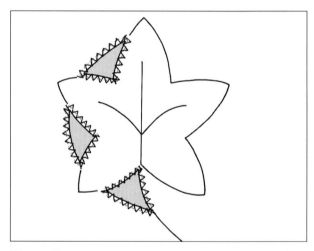

Fig 36B.

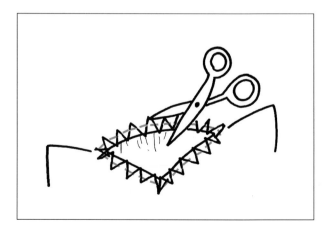

Fig 36C.

Step Three

Now that you have prepared the cutwork edge, making it strong and neat, you are ready to satin stitch the complete design.

Preparation

Cut a piece of Magic Fabric (Solvi) large enough to cover the design area. Pin the Magic Fabric to the wrong side of the fabric covering the design area. The Magic Fabric will give the machine an extra surface to feed through making satin stitching on an edge easy for the machine and you to handle. Fig 37A.

Machine Settings

> Zig -Zag
>
> Stitch Width: Average 3mm
>
> Stitch length: between 0.6mm and 0.4mm
>
> Tension: As for satin stitch

1. Satin stitch your design.

- Stitch from the background to the foreground. Take some time and study your chosen design, which areas are behind other areas? Example, the semi circle is behind the Ivy leaf, so you would stitch the semi circle first and then stitch the Ivy leaf. Stitching from the background to the foreground will not only give your finished work a professional finish it will take full advantage of oversewing as well, eliminating the need to tie off tail threads. Fig 37B.

- When stitching on the cutwork edge the majority of the stitch should fall on the fabric, with the stitch just going over the cutwork edge.

2. Once all stitching is complete, gently tear the Magic Fabric (Solvi) and the Fabric Stabiliser away from behind your work.

3. Rinse your work under luke warm running water to dissolve any residue of Magic Fabric.

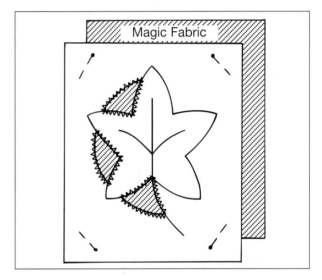

Fig 37A.

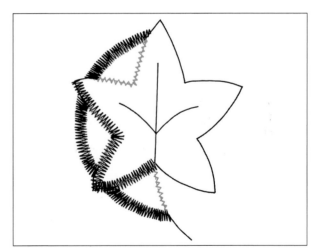

Fig 37B.

Edge Cutwork

Cutwork stitched onto an edge is naturally suited to collars and table linen. You can of course place cutwork onto the edge of anything. Of the seven designs in the book, five are suitable for placing on an edge. You will find the designs suitability for edge cutwork on the design idea pages in Chapter 12" Designs".

Collars

The collar is first stitched with the cutwork and then the garment is constructed. When cutwork is stitched onto a collar, you will be stitching through two layers of fabric, the upper and under collar, as well as through the interfacing, all of which are bonded (glued) together. For this reason garment patterns that have a front and back facing are best to work with. These types of garment patterns make the attachment of the collar to the garment simple and easy.

Preparation

1. Cut two collar pieces from your fabric

*   Cut one collar piece from iron on interfacing.

*   Cut one collar piece from Bonding (glue in the form of fabric) Trim the seam allowance away from the seam that attaches the collar to the garment.

2. Layer the above cut pieces as follows, Fig 38B.

    1: Fabric,wrong side facing up

    2: Bonding

    3: Interfacing, fusible side facing up

    4: Fabric right side facing up

3. Fuse the pieces together by ironing. Set the iron temperature to suit the fabric. Ensure they are fused together well.

4. Using a fabric marking pen, mark the seam allowance line around the edge of the collar. Fig 38C.

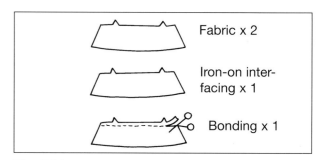

Fabric x 2

Iron-on inter-facing x 1

Bonding x 1

Fig 38A.

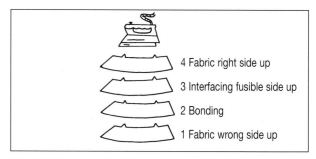

4 Fabric right side up

3 Interfacing fusible side up

2 Bonding

1 Fabric wrong side up

Fig 38B.

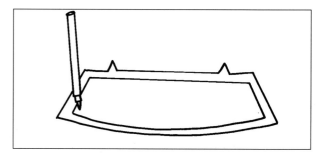

Fig 38C.

5. Transfer your design to the edge of the seam allowance. Fig 39 A.

Stitching

Because the collar is stabilised by the interfacing we will not need to use any other type of Fabric Stabiliser.

1. Stitch "Step One" of the cutwork technique around the areas to be cut out which will include every edge of the collar except the edge that attaches the collar to the garment. Fig 39B.

• Cut out the cutwork areas including the stitched collar edge.

2. Stitch "Step Two" of the cutwork technique around the cutwork areas. Including the collar edge.

• Trim any fraying fabric from the cutwork edge. Fig 39C.

Fig 39A.

Fig 39B.

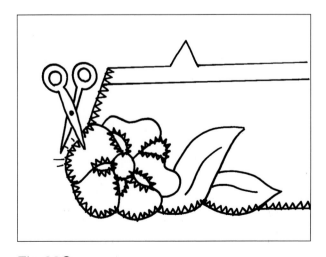

Fig 39C.

3. Cut a piece of Magic Fabric (Solvi) large enough so it will extend from the edge of the collar by least 2cm. Pin it to the wrong side of the collar. Fig 40A.

4. Stitch Step Three of the cutwork technique (satin stitch). Fig 40B.

5. Once all stitching is complete, gently tear the Magic Fabric (Solvi) away from behind your work. Rinse your work under luke warm running water to dissolve any residue of Magic Fabric.

6. Construct your garment.

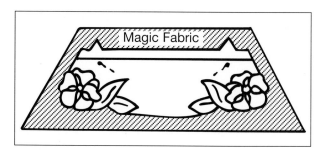

Fig 40A.

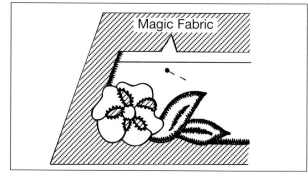

Fig 40B.

Single Layer Of Fabric Edge Cutwork

The following refers to table linen, bed linen, pockets and any cutwork stitched onto a single layer of fabric. The following diagrams are of a napkin.

Preparation

1. Cut out the article from your fabric, allowing a extra 1.5cm (5/8") of fabric on the edges where the cutwork will be applied.

2. Using a fabric marking pen, mark the seam allowance line on the edges to be cutworked. Fig 40C.

3. Transfer your design to the edges of the seam allowance. Fig 40D.

4. Iron the Fabric Stabiliser to the wrong side of your fabric, covering the design area. Fig 40D.

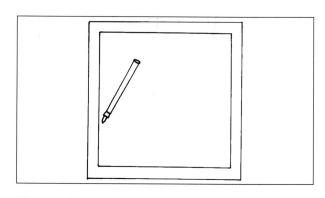

Fig 40 C.

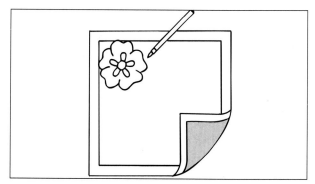

Fig 40 D.

NOTE: If you will be sewing a long row of stitching between cutwork design sections, example: the area in between two corner sections on a tablecloth, cut strips of Fabric Stabiliser to cover this area.

NOTE: If you are working on something large, such as a tablecloth, for ease of handling it is best to stitch a section at a time, example: one corner stitched completely at a time.

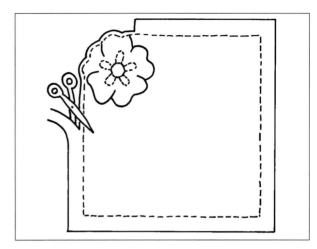

Fig 41A.

Stitching

1. Stitch "Step One" of the cutwork technique around the areas to be cut out which will include the edge

- Cut out the cutwork areas including the marked edge. Fig 41A.

2. Stitch "Step Two" of the cutwork technique around the cutwork areas. Including the edge.

- Trim any fraying fabric from the cutwork edge. Fig 41B.

3. Cut a piece of Magic Fabric (Solvi) large enough so it will extend from the edge at least 2cm. Pin it to the wrong side of the fabric. Fig 41C.

NOTE: If you will be sewing a long row of stitching between cutwork design sections, example: the area in between two corner sections on a tablecloth, cut strips of Magic Fabric to cover this area.

Fig 41B.

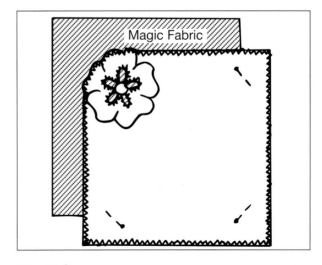

Fig 41C.

4. Stitch "Step Three" of the cutwork technique (satin stitch) Fig 42 A.

5. Once all stitching is completed, gently tear the Magic Fabric (Solvi) and the Fabric Stabiliser away from behind your work. Rinse your work under luke warm running water to dissolve any residue of Magic Fabric.

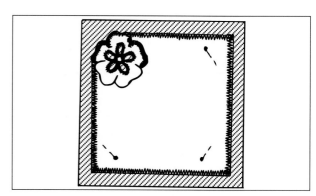

Fig 42A.

A Few Tips On Stitching Curves And Points On An Edge

To achieve a neat finish when stitching curves and points on a cutwork edge, the handling of the fabric is important. The main tip is to take your time and not rush the stitching.

Curves

The designs have been structured so that any curves that are on an edge are not too sharp. This will allow you in most cases to stitch the edge curves without the need to pivot.

If you do need to pivot on a curve the point where the needle is left down will often be off the edge of the fabric. For this reason it is important to pivot the fabric carefully so as not to move the fabric out of alignment with the stitching. Take your time and turn the hand wheel of your machine for the first stitch, after pivoting, to check that the stitch is aligned correctly with the previous stitching. Fig 42 B.

Pivot point is off the fabric

Fig 42B.

Points

Of the three methods of stitching points, standard, mitred and tapered, the standard and mitred are suitable to stitch on a cutwork edge. Because a tapered point has a very narrow stitch width it is unsuitable for edge cutwork.

The main trick in stitching points on an edge is to ensure the point is well covered by stitching.

DESCRIPTION:
The beauty of a Cutwork Edge is high lighted when placed against a contrasting colour. You can utilize plain and printed fabrics to achieve this stunning effect.

DESIGN:
Alpine Flower

SECTION:
D

TECHNIQUES:
Edge Cutwork, page 44
Zig-Zag Outline Stitch, page 36
Standard Point on an edge,
page 53

DESCRIPTION:
A traditional feminine style is created with pastel pink linen, an easy to handle fabric that is ideal for beginners.

DESIGN:
Mock Orange

SECTION:
Collar - Section C
Pocket - Section D

TECHNIQUES:
Edge Cutwork, page 44
Insertion Cutwork, cotton netting, page 57
Outline Stitch, page 35

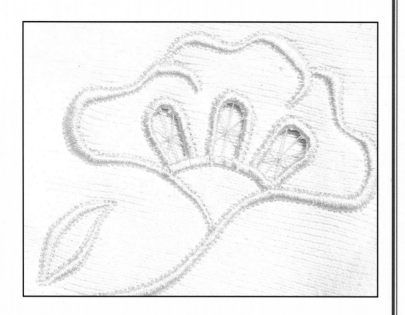

DESCRIPTION:

Cutwork can be stitched on a wide range of fabrics including knits. The fibres of mohair and cotton complement Cutwork beautifully as shown on these two knitted garments.

Cream Knit

DESIGN:
Rock Rose

SECTION:
C

TECHNIQUES:
Knitted fabrics, page 56
Variable width Satin Stitch, page 34
Outline Stitch, page 35
Fine Richelieu Bars, page 59
Tapered point, page 33

Blue Knit

DESIGN:
Pansy

SECTION:
D

TECHNIQUES:
Insertions, page 57
Design Outline, page 36

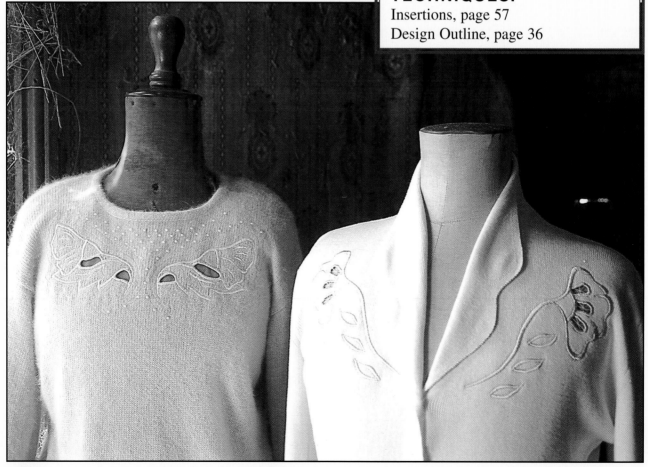

Standard Point

A standard point is stitched completely with the same stitch width.

1. Stitch all the way to the end of the point leaving the needle down in the fabric at the outside edge of the point. Fig 43A.

2. Pivot, so you will be stitching horizontally across the point.

   Manually turning the hand wheel of your machine, stitch 3 to 5 stitches horizontally across the point. Fig 43B.

4. Leave the needle down on the outside edge of the point, pivot so you are aligned to sew the next row of stitching.

   It is important that this first stitch, stitches onto the fabric. Turning the hand wheel manually will allow you to ensure that the stitch connects with the fabric. Fig 43C.

5. Continue stitching, if you feel the stitch is bunching up, gently pull the fabric to help the machine feed the stitching through.

Mitred Point

If your sewing machine stitch width adjustments are made by increments ie: increased by 0.5mm at a time you will not be able to achieve an even flow to a mitred point, in which case it will be better for you to stitch the standard point.

1. Stitch all the way to the end of the point, keeping the angle of the stitch in line with the point. leave the needle down on the outside edge of the point. Fig 43D.

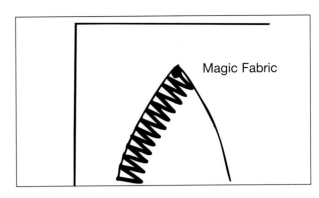

Fig 43A.

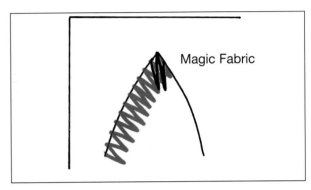

Fig 43B.

Fig 43C.

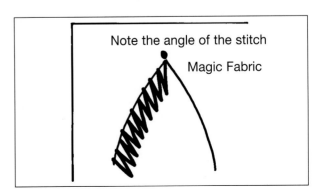

Fig 43D.

2. Raise the pressure foot and pivot so you are aligned to sew the next row of stitching.

3. Decrease the stitch width to 0.5mm

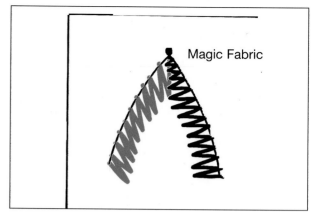

Fig 44A.

4. Raise the needle and re-align the fabric so the needle goes into the point it last came out of. Fig 44A.

5. It is important that this first stitch, stitches onto the fabric. Turning the hand wheel manually will allow you to ensure that the stitch connects with the fabric.

6. With your hand on the stitch width dial start stitching, increasing the width as you sew. If you feel the stitch is bunching up, gently pull the fabric to help the machine feed the stitching through.

Note: Stitch slowly yet increase the stitch width rapidly, you want the last stitch that oversews the first row of stitching to be of an equal width to that of the first.

Coloured Stitching

Cutwork is traditionally stitched in the same coloured thread as the fabric. We can break from the obvious and stitch our design in a single contrast colour or multi-colours. Adding colour to your cutwork will give it a new look and that look can change with the colours chosen.

Single Contrast Colour Stitching

When selecting a contrasting coloured thread keep within the tone of the fabric. For example, pastel shaded fabrics such as light blues, pinks etc, should be stitched with contrasting pastel coloured threads. Strong coloured fabrics such as reds, navy, etc should be stitched with strong contrasting coloured threads. If you use a pastel thread such as white on a black fabric you will find the overall finish unsatisfactory as any tiny unevenness in the stitching will be visible. It is also difficult for a pale thread to cover the strong coloured fabric beneath it.

"Technique"

- The stitching technique is the same as for standard cutwork. Stitch all Three Steps of the cutwork in the chosen coloured thread.

Multi Coloured Stitching

You can use as many different colours as the design calls for, the look of the finished cutwork will vary with the colours chosen. As for single contrast colour stitching select colours that are in the same tone as your fabric, pale coloured threads on pale coloured fabric, strong coloured threads on strong coloured fabrics.

Technique

- Stitch Step One and Step Two in the same colour as the fabric and change to the coloured threads for Step Three. For example, if the fabric is white, Step One and Step Two would be stitched in white thread, Step Three would then be stitched in your chosen coloured threads.

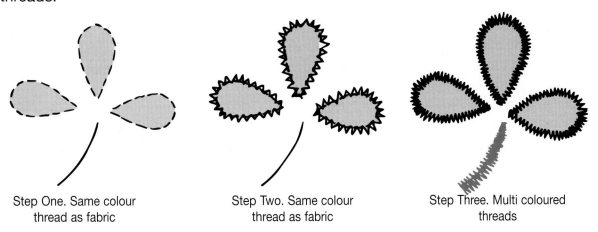

Step One. Same colour thread as fabric

Step Two. Same colour thread as fabric

Step Three. Multi coloured threads

Cutwork On Knits

Stitching cutwork onto knitted fabric is easy and creates a wonderful finish, at times a quilted look is achieved. You can embroider cutwork onto any medium/light to medium/heavy weight tightly knitted fabric. The tightness of the knit is important as the cutwork area is stitched three times. If the knit is loose and open the stitching will not have enough fibre's to hold onto. Utilising ready made garments offers an easy and wide selection of various types of knits. If you happen to be a machine knitter, cutwork is ideal to use as an embellishment on your knitted creations. Good quality T-Shirting and fleecy backed knits, which have body and strength are also ideal to use.

Adding Stability To The Cutwork Areas

Because knitted fabrics stretch, adding either an insertion fabric or Richelieu bars to the cutwork areas will add extra stability to the embroidered area. For instructions on insertion fabrics please refer to page 57 " Insertion Cutwork". For instructions on Richelieu bars please refer to Chapter 8 "Richelieu Bars"

Stabilising

It is very important to stabilise knits to prevent the fabric stretching. Fabric Stabiliser (iron on paper) is the easiest method of stabilising knitted fabrics. If you are working on a fleecy backed fabric, test on an off cut to see that when the stabiliser is removed it does not remove the fleece with it. This can happen, especially on economically priced fabrics. If there is a problem, simply iron the stabiliser on very lightly using a cool iron (permanent press).

Stitching

Because of the nature of knit fabrics the stitch sinks into the fabric, for this reason you will need to make the stitch wider when stitching "Steps Two and Three" of the cutwork process. Listed below you will find stitch settings for medium weight knit fabric, keep in mind if you are working on a lighter or heavier knit these settings will need to be adjusted accordingly.

Machine Settings For The Three Steps Of Cutwork

For detailed instructions on the "Three Steps Of Cutwork" please refer to chapter 3.

Step One	Step Two	Step Three
Straight Stitch	Zig-Zag	Zig-Zag
Stitch width: 0	Stitch width: 2.5mm	Stitch width: 4mm
Stitch length: 1.5mm	Stitch length: 0.8mm	Stitch Length: Between
Tension: Normal	Tension: Normal	0.6mm and 4mm
		Tension: As for satin stitch

Insertion Cutwork

The inserting of sheer fabrics behind cutwork adds an elegant finish to fashion and home decor items. Insertion fabrics not only add that something special to your work, the technique also has practical purposes. Insertions can be used when a design is positioned on a fashion item in areas where bra straps may show, inserting a fabric behind the cutwork will disguise any undergarments. The technique is also used to add stability to the cutwork areas when stitching on knitted fabrics.

Insertion Fabric As A Lining

Your insertion fabric can be placed behind your cutwork in the simple form of a lining. This technique is suitable for items where it is possible to apply a lining such as, bodice fronts and backs, sleeves, pockets, quilts and cushion covers. To apply a lining it is simply a matter of cutting the lining from your chosen insertion fabric and applying it to the article during construction. Lace, organza, chiffon and cotton netting are all ideal to use when inserting a fabric as a lining.

Insertion Fabric Stitched Into The Cutwork

Insertion fabric can also be stitched behind your work as you stitch the "Three Steps Of Cutwork". By stitching the insertion fabrics in this way it eliminates any bulk of insertion fabric at the back of your work. Lace, chiffon and cotton netting are all ideal to use as insertion fabric for this method. Organza is unsuitable as it tends to perforate when satin stitched on.

Stitching

For detailed instructions on " The Three Steps Of Cutwork" please refer to Chapter 3

1. Transfer your chosen design to your article.

2. Stabilise the fabric.

3. Stitch " Step One" of the cutwork technique.

4. Stitch " Step Two " of the cutwork technique.

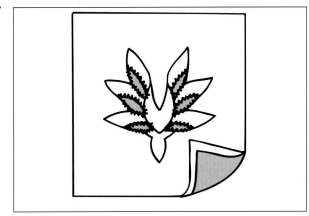

Fig 47 A.

5. Cut a piece of insertion fabric large enough to cover your design area. Pin and machine tack it in place to the wrong side of your work. Fig 48A.

Note: It is not necessary to use Magic Fabric (Solvi) behind your work as the insertion will take it's place.

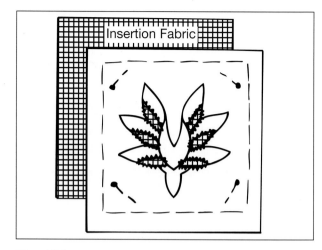

Fig 48A.

6. Stitch " Step Three" of the cutwork technique.

7. Stitch an outline stitch, either straight stitch or zig-zag, around the satin stitch, this adds extra stability to the insertion fabric. Fig 48B.

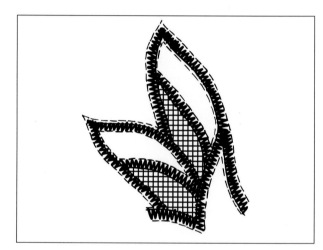

Fig 48B.

8. Using embroidery scissors trim the insertion fabric away from all areas except the cutwork areas. For extra stability when trimming around the cutwork areas leave approximately 3mm (1/8") extending out from the outline stitch. Fig 48C.

9. Remove the Fabric Stabiliser from behind your work.

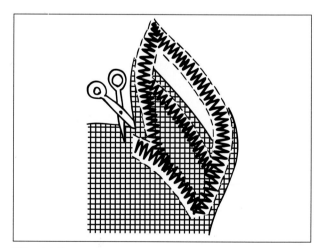

Fig 48C.

Richelieu Bars

The fun and ease of stitching this decorative finish is quite amazing! Using a straight stitch and zig-zag, various patterns can be formed by the Richelieu bars. They may be incorporated into any cutwork area and add extra stability especially on knit fabrics. There are two types of Richelieu bars, a fine and a heavy, they can be stitched singularly or the two can be combined with-in the one design. The technique of applying the Richelieu bars to the cutwork will vary a little depending on whether you chose to form a basic or an intricate pattern. If you are creating an intricate pattern with the bars please refer to " Intricate Patterns" page 62 after you have read the instructions below.

Fine Richelieu Bars

For detailed instructions on the " Three Steps Of Cutwork" please refer to Chapter 3.

Formed by a single row of straight stitch the fine Richelieu bar is the quicker of the two methods to stitch. It is ideal to use when stitching intricate patterns and may also be combined with the heavy Richelieu bars.

1. Transfer your chosen design to your article.

2. Stabilise the fabric.

3. Stitch "Step One" of the cutwork technique.

4. Stitch "Step Two" of the cutwork technique.

5. Cut a piece of Magic Fabric (Solvi) large enough to cover the design area. Pin it to the back of your work. Fig 53B

6. Set your machine to:

Machine Settings

Straight stitch

Stitch width: 0

Stitch length: 1.5

Tension: normal

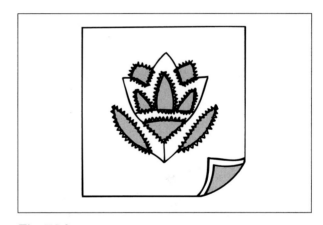

Fig 53A.

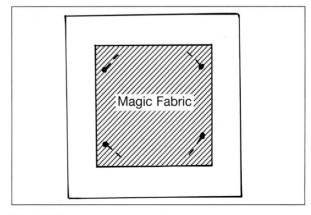

Fig 53B.

7. Start on the fabric at the edge of the cutwork area. Reverse stitch a couple of stitches to secure the sewing.

8. Stitch across the cutwork area to your finishing point, anchoring the stitch on the fabric. Fig 54A.

Note: After stitching the first Richelieu bar, cut the tail threads off so they do not get entangled under your work.

9. Stitching on the fabric, sew to your next starting point. Fig 54B.

10. Continue stitching steps 8 and 9 until you have completed the Richelieu bars for that cutwork area. Once finished, reverse stitch to secure the row of sewing. Cut the tail threads. Fig 54 C.

11. Stitch "Step Three" of the cutwork technique. Fig 54D.

12. Remove the Fabric Stabiliser and rinse your work under luke warm running water to dissolve any residue of Magic Fabric.

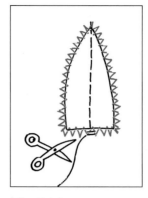

Fig 54A.

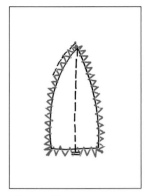

Fig 54B.

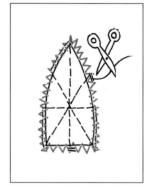

Fig 54C.

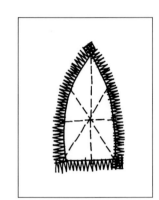

Fig 54D.

Heavy Richelieu Bars

Formed by zig-zaging over two rows of straight stitching the heavy Richelieu bar will add a bolder finish and is stronger than the fine bars.

1. Transfer your chosen design to your article.

2. Stabilise the fabric.

Fig 54E.

3. Stitch "Step One" of the cutwork technique.

4. Stitch "Step Two" of the cutwork technique.

5. Cut a piece of Magic Fabric (Solvi) large enough to cover the design area. Pin it to the back of your work. Fig 55A.

6. Set your machine to:

Machine Settings

    Straight stitch

    Stitch width: 0

    Stitch length: 1.5

    Tension: normal

7. Start on the fabric at the edge of the cutwork area. Reverse stitch a couple of stitches to secure the sewing.

8. Stitch across the cutwork area to your finishing point, sew two stitches onto the fabric to anchor the Richelieu bar. Fig 55B.

Note: After stitching the first Richelieu bar, cut the tail threads off so they do not get entangled under your work.

9. Pivot and stitch another row of straight stitch as close as possible to the previous row of straight stitching. Sew two stitches onto the fabric to anchor the Richelieu bar. Fig 55C.

10. Set your machine to:

Machine Settings

    Zig - Zag

    Stitch width: 1.5

    Stitch length: 0.8

    Tension: normal

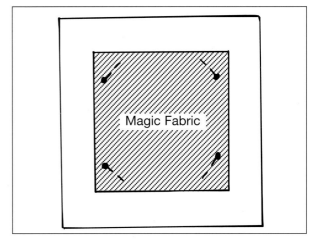

Fig 55A.

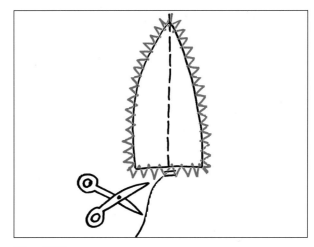

Fig 55B.

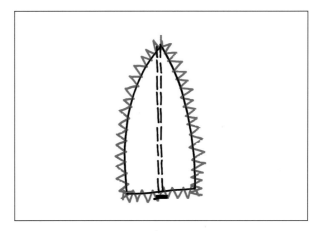

Fig 55C.

11. Zig - zag over the two rows of straight stitching. Fig 56A.

12. Set your machine back to straight stitch as in step 6. Stitching on the fabric, sew to your next starting point. Fig 56B.

13. Continue stitching steps 8 through to 12 until you have completed the Richelieu bars for that cutwork area. Once finished, reverse stitch to secure the row of sewing. Cut the tail threads. Fig 56C.

14. Stitch "Step Three" of the cutwork technique. Fig 56D.

15. Remove the Fabric Stabiliser and rinse your work under luke warm running water to dissolve any residue of Magic Fabric.

Note: The zig-zag used is slightly open, this keeps the bars taut between the cutwork edges. If you were to stitch the zig-zag as dense as a satin stitch, the bars would stretch creating an untidy finish.

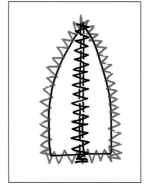

Fig 56A.

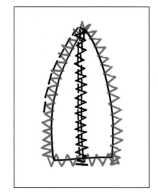

Fig 56B.

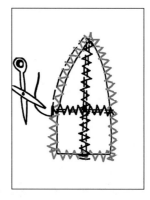

Fig 56C.

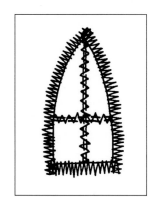

Fig 56D.

Intricate Patterns Formed By Richelieu Bars

Stitched Onto Vanish-a-Way

Any type of intricate pattern may be formed with the Richelieu bars. To achieve a satisfactory result, stitch guide lines will be needed. Vanish-a-Way is ideal to use as it is firm enough to draw guide lines onto. Once the stitching is completed the Vanish-A-Way is ironed, turning it to a powder which can be brushed away from the stitching. Because of the nature of Vanish-A-Way it is best removed prior to satin stitching "Step Three" of the cutwork technique. The following instructions will take you through the technique of creating Richelieu bars on Vanish-a-Way. You will also find at the end of this chapter patterns which can be traced onto the Vanish-A-Way and used when stitching Richelieu bars.

1. Transfer your chosen design to your article.

2. Stabilise the fabric.

3. Stitch "Step One" of the cutwork technique.

4. Stitch "Step Two" of the cutwork technique.

5. Cut a piece of Vanish-A-Way large enough to cover the design area. Pin it to the back of your work. Fig 57 B.

6. From the right side of your work using a blue fabric marking pen (water erasable) mark your Richelieu stitch guide lines onto the Vanish-A-Way. Fig 57 C.

Note: If using the Richelieu patterns at the end of this chapter simply place your work over the chosen pattern, line the pattern up within a cutwork area and trace the pattern onto the Vanish-A-Way.

7. Stitch the Richelieu bars Fig 57 D.

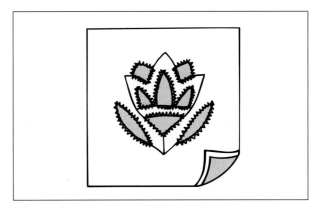

Fig 57A.

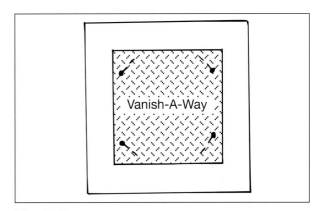

Fig 57B.

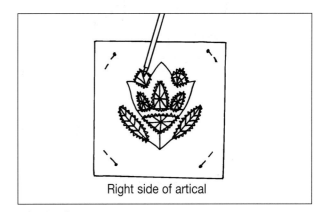

Right side of artical

Fig 57C.

Fig 57D.

8. Using a DRY iron set to cotton, iron the Vanish-A-Way from the back of your work (wrong side). It will turn brown, don't worry this is suppose to happen, the darker you iron it the easier it will be removed. Using an old tooth-brush, gently brush the stitching to remove all residue of the Vanish-A-Way. Fig 58A.

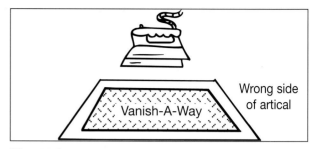

Fig 58A.

9. Cut a piece of Magic Fabric (Solvi) large enough to cover the design area. Pin it to the back of your work. Fig 58B.

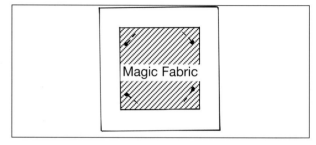

Fig 58B.

10. Stitch "Step Three" of the cutwork technique. Fig 58C.

11. Remove the Fabric Stabiliser and rinse your work under luke warm running water to dissolve any residue of Magic Fabric.

Fig 58C.

Tips On Stitching Leaf Veins And Spider Web Centres

Leaf Veins

When stitching leaf veins, stitch the centre vein using a heavy Richelieu bar. This will give the outer veins a solid surface to anchor onto, preventing them from moving. If the veins are stitched using only a fine Richelieu bar the outer veins will move, creating an untidy finish. Fig 58D.

Spider Web Centre

There are two methods to create a centre to spider web Richelieu patterns.

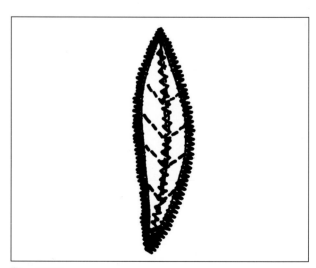

Fig 58D.

Method One

Method one is stitched using the fine Richelieu bar. If we stitched from the centre, out, we would end up with the tail threads on the outer edge of our centre piece. This would leave us with a unsightly knot showing. To avoid this we will be stitching from the outer edge into the centre.

1. Using the fine Richelieu bar, start on the outer edge of the spider wed centre, bring the bobbin thread to the top of your work, stitch around the outer edge once. Fig 59A.

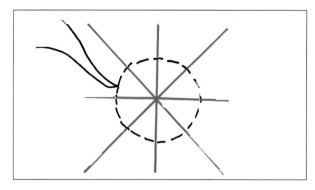

Fig 59A.

2. Lay the two tail threads across the centre of the spider wed, stitch another two circular rows towards the centre. Fig 59B.

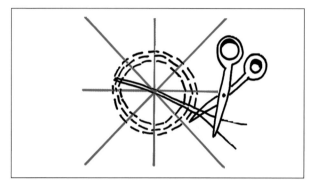

Fig 59B.

3. Cut the tail threads.

4. Continue stitching towards the centre, pivoting sharply. Fig 59C.

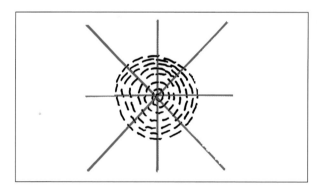

Fig 59C.

5. Once all stitching is complete take the top tail thread to the back of your work and tie the threads off, cut the tail threads leaving 0.5cm from the knot for added strength.

Method Two

This method is very quick and easy, Simply hand stitch a sequin and bead to the centre of your spider web. Knot the tail thread at the back of your work and leave 0.5cm of thread from the knot for added strength. Fig 59D.

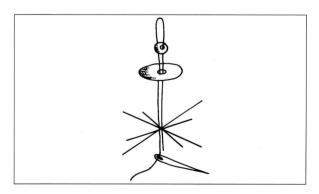

Fig 59D.

▼ 65

Patterns For Richelieu Bars

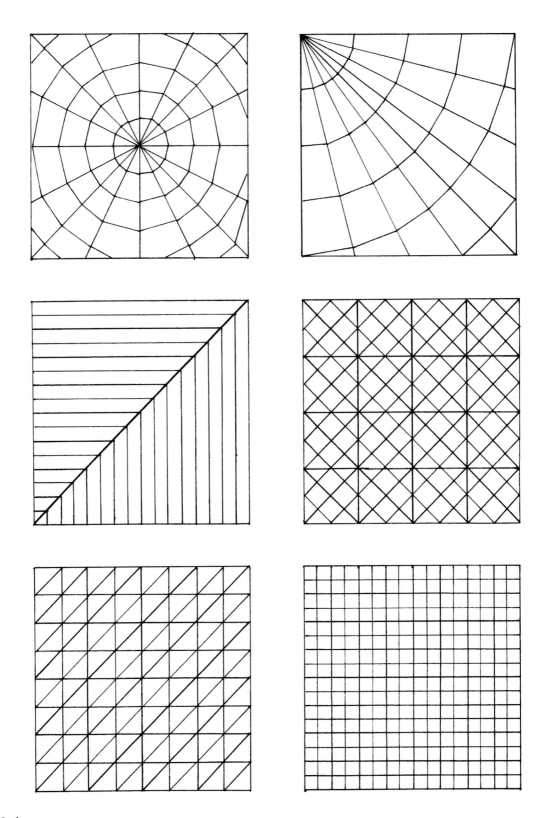

Fig 60 A.

Transferring The Designs

Remember to mark all areas to be cutout. A simple + is fine to use.

For ease of use first photocopy or trace onto paper the design sections you wish to use.

There are several methods you can use to transfer the design lines onto your fabric. The method you use will depend on the equipment you have available as well as whether you are working on light or dark coloured fabric.

Transfer Pencil

Transfer pencils are generally available from haberdashery (Notions) stores and come in either a pink or green lead. Transfer pencils are unsuitable for dark coloured fabrics as the lines will not show. Do be aware that the transfer lines will be permanent on most fabrics. If you iron the transfer on with a hot iron the transfer lines will be dark and they may show through light coloured stitching. I suggest to iron the transfer on using an iron setting of permanent press, this will mean the transfer lines will iron on light in colour, so the lines will be hidden when stitched over. If the faint lines are hard to see they can than be drawn over using a blue wash out marking pen. Also keep in mind that the design will iron on mirror imaged, eg. when you trace a left hand design, it will transfer onto your project as a right hand side design.

To use: Trace the design lines onto tracing paper. Position and pin the traced design onto your article with the tracing face down onto the right side of the fabric, press using a cool iron. Do not push the iron across the paper as this tends to move the paper, resulting in a blurred line instead of a crisp neat line. Remove the tracing paper.

TIP: The chemicals in iron on transfer pencils are affected by exposure to air. This can result in them not working, iron as you may, they will not transfer . The simple solution is to sharpen the pencil each time you use it.

Dressmaker carbon paper

This is the best method for dark coloured fabrics as the design lines will be clearly visible. The only disadvantage of using dressmakers carbon paper is that the lines can rub off with excessive handling. If you are working on a large article to avoid this from occurring, either trace and stitch a section at a time or stitch over all the design lines using a straight stitch, length 1.5 in a visible thread colour.

To use: Work on a hard even surface for best results. Place the dressmakers carbon on the right side of your fabric, place the design on top of the dressmakers carbon paper, pin in position. If working on a woven fabric trace the design lines using a hard pencil . If you are working on a knit fabric you will need to use a tracing wheel.

Water Erasable Blue Marking Pen

These pens are ideal to use as the marks on the fabric will wash out in water. They are available in a heavy and fine tip, the fine tip gives you a definite line to follow. If you are working on a large project that will take a few sewing sessions to complete, store your unfinished item in a plastic bag. This will prevent the lines from fading due to moisture in the air. Also when ironing do not use steam as again this will cause the lines to fade.

To Use: Place the design under the fabric against the wrong side. From the right side of the fabric trace the design onto your article.

Vanishing Pens

Generally available in pink or purple. These pens are fine to use if stitching your project in one session as they will vanish within 48 to 72 hours. If stitching a large project which may take more than one session, use one of the other means of transferring your design so the design lines do not vanish before you have completed your project.

To Use: Place the design under the fabric against the wrong side. From the right side of the fabric trace the design onto your article.

Light Box

In most cases if you are working on a light coloured fabric you will be able to see the design lines through the fabric to trace from. If you are unable to clearly see the design lines through the fabric a light source coming from behind the fabric will solve the problem. If you have a light box as part of your creative equipment, it is ideal to use. Now I know most of us do not have one of these wonderful things, why I don't know as I could not live without mine. Don't despair as you can make a temporary light box using a pane of glass or perspex and a strong light.

To make a temporary light box: You will need : glass or perspex - a strong light - two flat surfaces ie: chairs or boxes.

Place the glass or perspex securely between two flat surfaces, you can use chairs or boxes of even height. Place the light under the glass pointing upwards. You now have a light box. To use your light box place your design on the class, pin your fabric over the top of the design and using a blue wash out marking pen or vanishing pen trace the design onto the fabric.

DESCRIPTION:

The combination of gold colours, metallic thread and Richelieu Bars create a royal finish to this cushion.

DESIGN:

Lotus

SECTION:

B

TECHNIQUES:

Richelieu Bars, page 59
Spider Web Centre, page 64
Outlining the design, page 36
Metallic thread, page 14

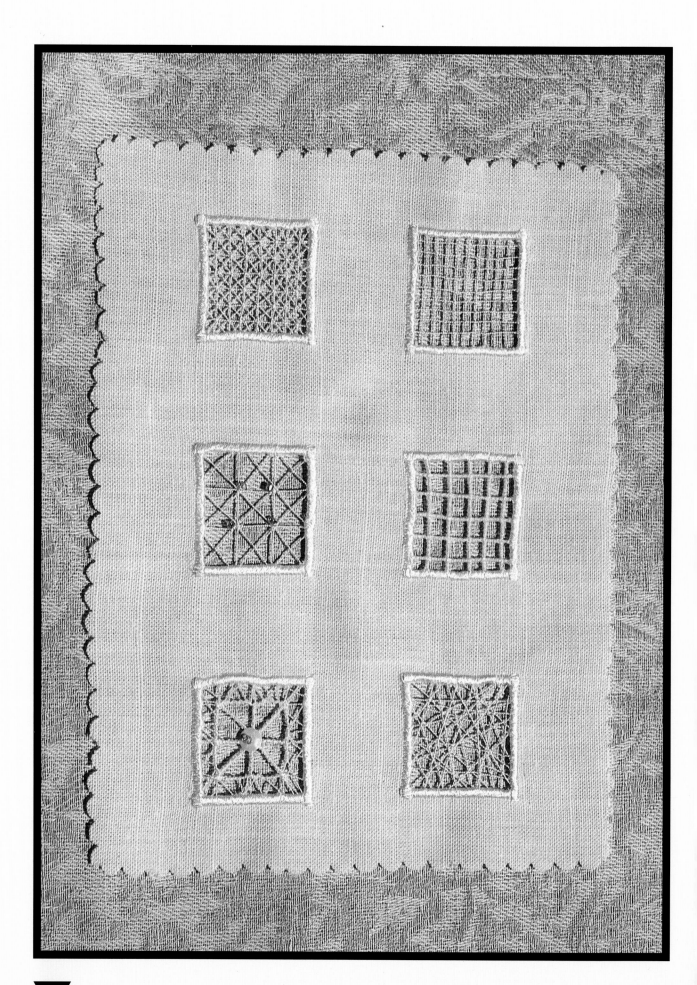

DESCRIPTION:
A simple summer blouse is transformed into "Something Special" by adding a touch of cutwork.

DESIGN:
Ivy

SECTION:
B

TECHNIQUES:
Heavy Richelieu Bars, page 60
Tapered Point, page 33

Design Placement

Where you place your chosen design on your article is as important as the design choice itself. Because each of the seven designs are made up of sections you will find a design to fit just about any area on fashion and home decor items. In chapter 12 "Designs" you will find design ideas which show you just some of the possibilities in design placement onto bed and table linen, quilts and fashion items. Don't be afraid to experiment as this is half the fun, below are some guidelines to follow when deciding where to place your cutwork design.

Placement Tips For Fashion Items

- Hold the selected garment section up to your body to see how the cutwork will fit in with the fall of the fabric.

- Avoid placement in areas where bra straps may show or to disguise bra straps insert a fabric ie: chiffon behind the design. Please refer to page 57 "Insertions" for stitching technique.

- If your cutwork is high on a front bodice and your garment requires shoulder pads be aware that the shoulder pads may show through the cutwork. This can be overcome when cutwork is on a jacket by, wearing the shoulder pads in the blouse that is to be worn with the jacket, or if the jacket is lined attaching the shoulder pads to the inside of the jacket, so the lining is between the shoulder pads and the cutwork.

Placement Tips For Home Decor Items

- When planning a table linen centre or doylie centre, keep in mind what may be placed on the artical, in the centre. For example a dinner cloth will require a large centre area for placing of condiments etc. Having a reasonably large area will avoid the centre cutwork from being hidden by such things.

- When planning table linen lay the cloth on the table before deciding on the placement of your cutwork. You will then be able to confidently plan the centre cutwork as well as any edge cutwork.

- When centralising a cutwork design, use a fabric marking pen to mark the vertical and horizontal centre lines on the fabric. This will give you a true guide to centre your design.

Combining The Design Sections

The seven designs in this book are each made up of sections. These sections can be stitched singularly or combined together to create a larger design. This allows you to add your own creativeness to your cutwork and makes each design very versatile. A combined design can be a square, a rectangle, a circle, an oval or just about any shape your project requires. When combining the design sections it is best to plan them on paper before transferring the design onto your article. I use butchers paper for this as it is inexpensive and big enough to create a large scale design on. You will find the designs as well as design ideas in chapter 12 "Designs".

The following information will give you some guidelines to follow when combining the design sections.

Combining a Single Section

You can take a single section and repeat it to form a larger design.

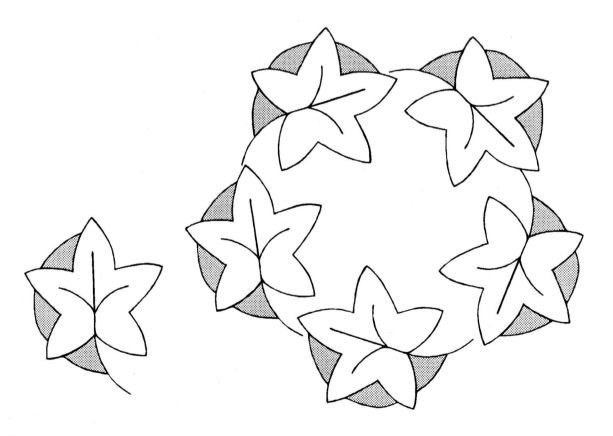

Combining More Than One Section

You can also take two or more sections of a design and combine them together to form a larger design.

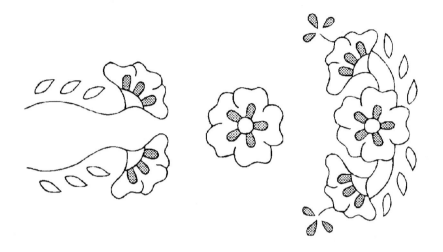

A Few Tips

- Photocopy several copies of the design sections you wish to use. You can then play around with the copies and see how they fit in together before you start tracing them onto butchers paper.

- Centre fold the paper to create accurate mirror images. Fig 70 A + 70B.

- Be careful not to place the designs sections too close together. You will need a minimum space of 0.5cm to allow for the width of the stitching, a little larger space is even better with most designs. This does not mean that stitching lines cannot join, the stems of the Ivy are meant to go together, yet if you were to join the leaves you would not only confuse the design, but also create an area of bulky stitching. Fig 70C + 70D.

- Trace your garment pattern piece onto the butchers paper and then trace your chosen design in position. You will be guaranteed a perfect placement.

- One of those wonderful light boxes are ideal to work with when tracing your designs. You will find information on making your own temporary light box on page 68.

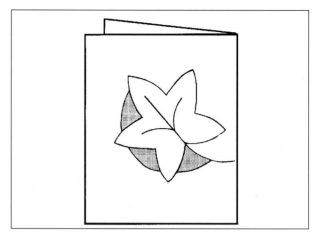

Fig 70A.

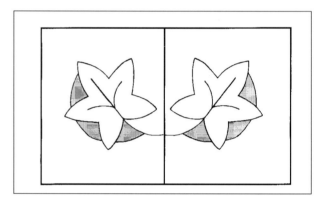

Fig 70B.

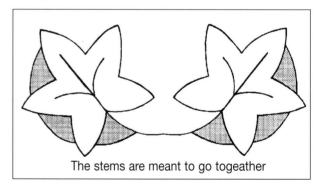

The stems are meant to go togeather

Fig 70C.

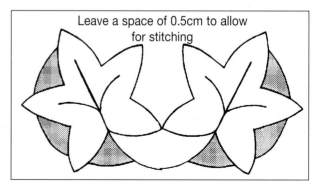

Leave a space of 0.5cm to allow for stitching

Fig 70D.

DESIGNS

From traditional to modern,

from quick and easy

to the creative masterpiece.

I have designed the following cutwork designs with all tastes in mind. Whether you be a traditional romantic, a modern dramatic or somewhere inbetween you will find something to suit your style.

The seven designs are made up of sections, these sections can be stitched singularly or combined together to create a larger design. Stitched singularly you can cutwork collars, pockets, sleeves, cushions, napkins or any small project. Combined together each design can be expanded to stitch quilts, table and bed linen, fronts and backs of blouses and jackets and made to fit just about any project you have in mind. Combining the design sections allows you to add your own creativeness to your cutwork as well as making the designs very versatile.

You will find ideas for combining the design in chapter 11 "Combining The Design Sections" and ideas for applying the designs to various articles on the following pages.

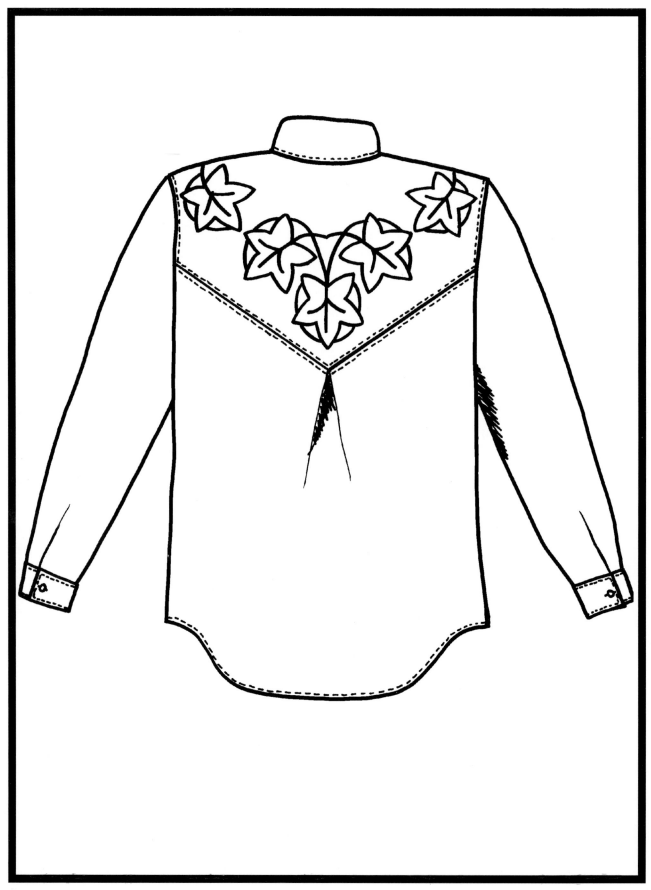

Fig 79 A.

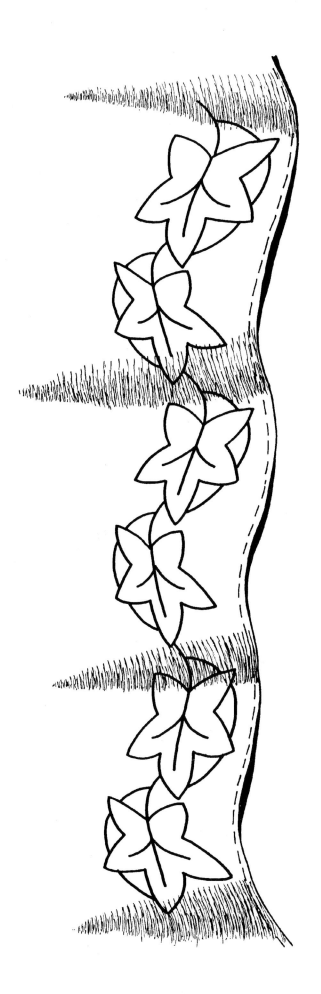

IVY

The simplicity of this design makes it ideal to create a first time project.

Start with the napkins and finish with the tablecloth to match.

I designed the ivy with the first time cutworker in mind. You will find it quick and simple to stitch, it will teach you the principles of stitching from the background to the foreground, stitching curves and points as well as steps one, two and three.

The cutwork areas are large enough to comfortably apply Richelieu bars or insertion fabrics. A great design to play and experiment with. You will find photos of table linen and a blouse stitched with the Ivy design on pages 24 and 72.

Design Ideas Ivy

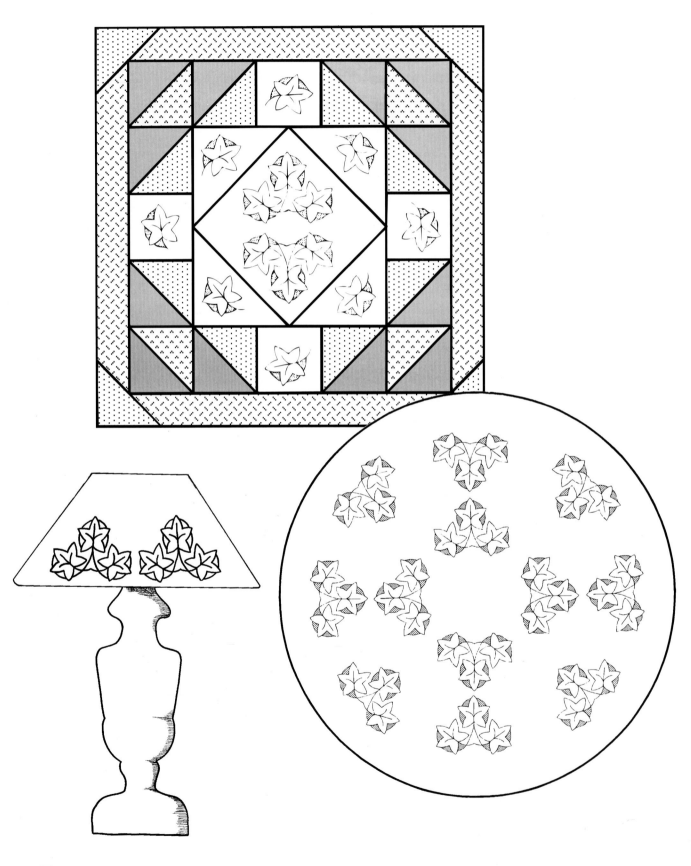

Design Ideas Ivy

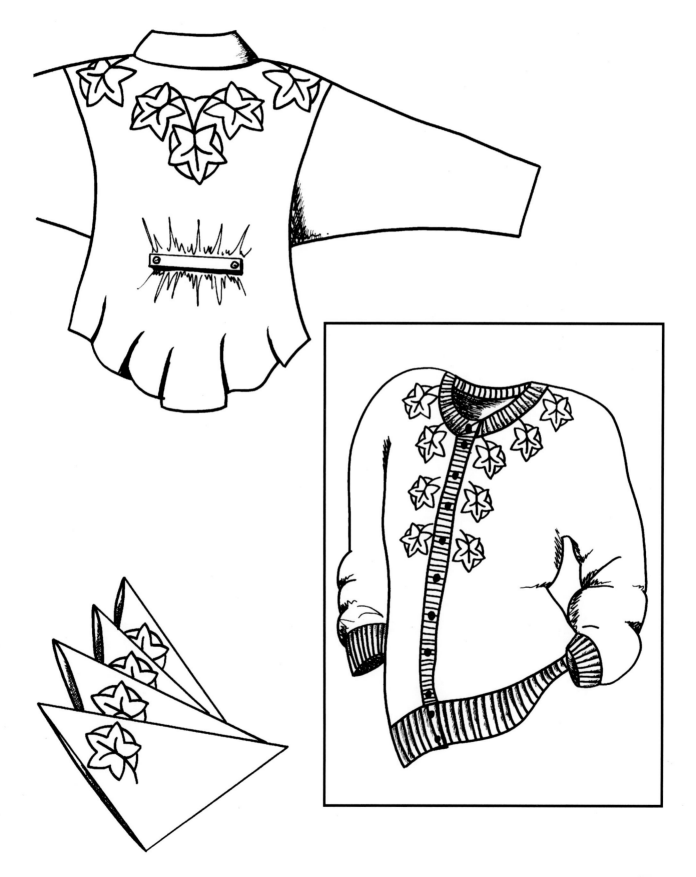

Ivy Section A

Note: the Ivy is unsuitable for edge cutwork

CUTWORK AREAS

Ivy Section B
Left and Right

CUTWORK AREAS

Alpine Flower

The Alpine flower has been designed for cutworking on an edge, whether you decide to stitch a simple doily or that special occasion tablecloth the beauty of the alpine flower will carry it on through the centuries as a true heirloom.

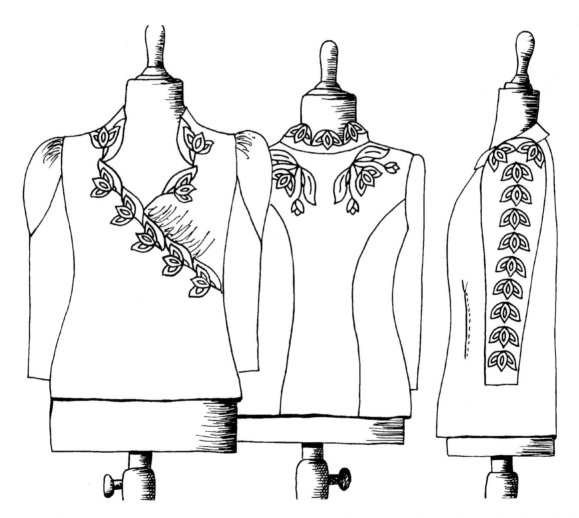

Working cutwork onto an edge as shown in chapter 4 is simple to do and adds that extra touch of elegance to any item. The child's dress on page 49 shows you the beauty of the edge as it stands against a contrasting coloured background fabric.

Although designed for working on an edge you may also utilise this design to be stitched within the centre of an article . The following design ideas show you how it wil look on an edge or placed elswhere on your project.

Design Ideas Alpine Flower

Design Ideas Alpine Flower

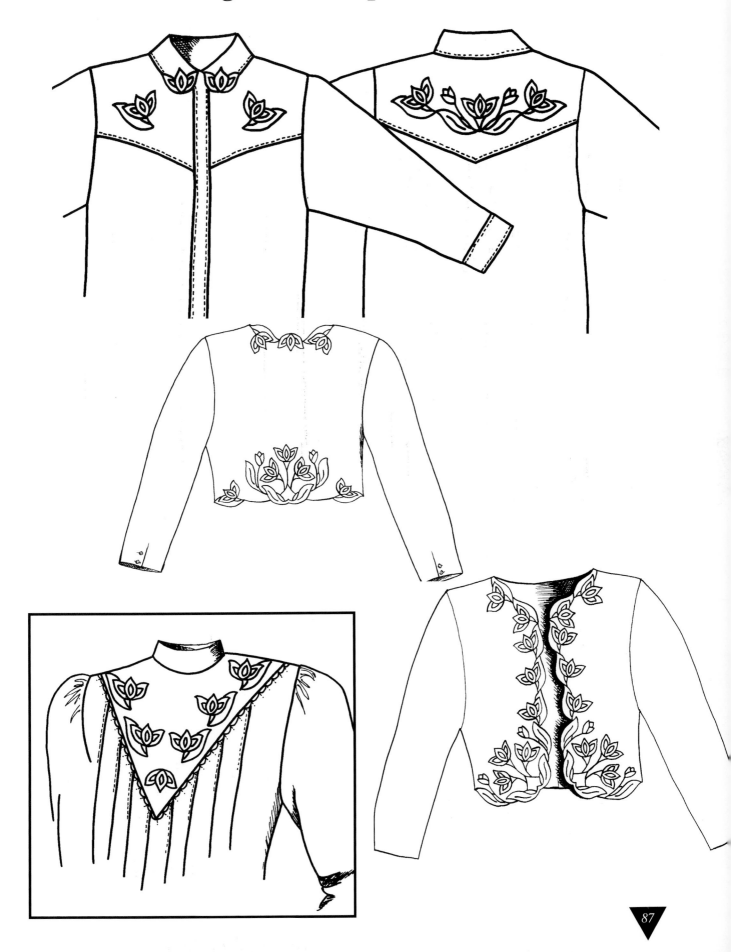

Alpine Flower Section A

NOTE; All sections suitable for edge cutwork

CUTWORK AREAS

Alpine Flower Section B

☐ *CUTWORK AREAS*

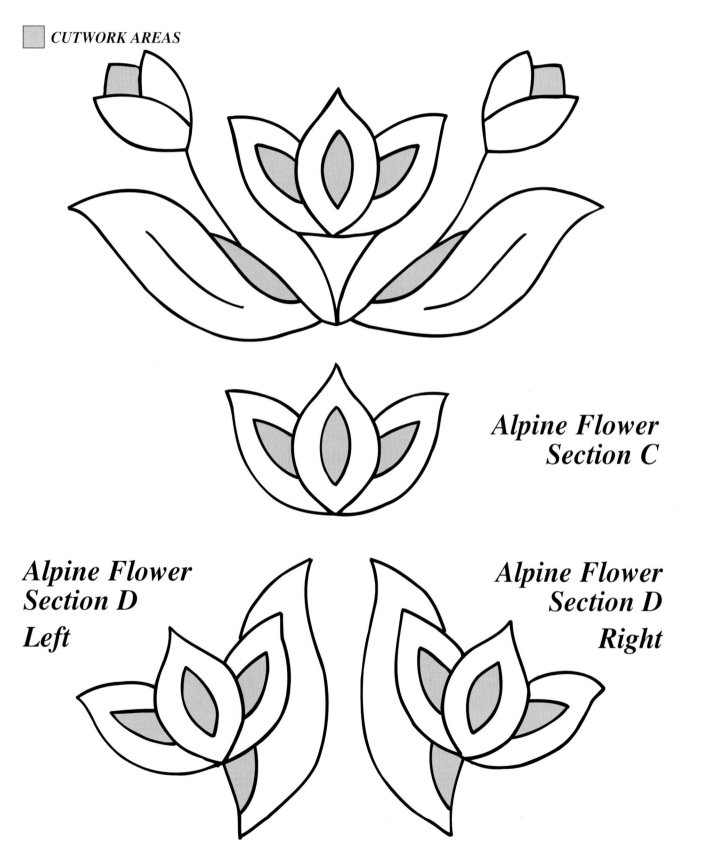

*Alpine Flower
Section C*

*Alpine Flower
Section D
Left*

*Alpine Flower
Section D
Right*

Pansy

Who can resist the happy face of a pansy! Stitched on an edge or inserted, this design will always put a smile on our own faces.

As the Pansy is a large design it is well suited to home decor items or that fashion item that you wish to make a statement with. The pansy is also a great design to stitch in multi coloured threads.

Although designed for working on an edge you may also utilise this design to be stitched with-in the centre of an article. The knitwear on page 52 shows you this simple technique. For inspiration turn the page to see design ideas using the Pansy.

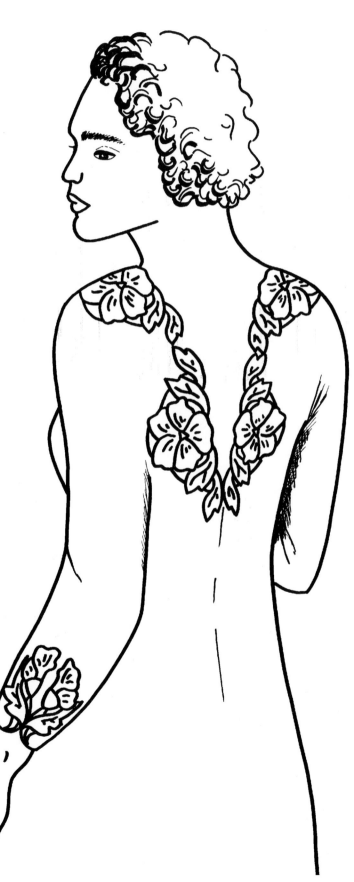

Design Ideas Pansy

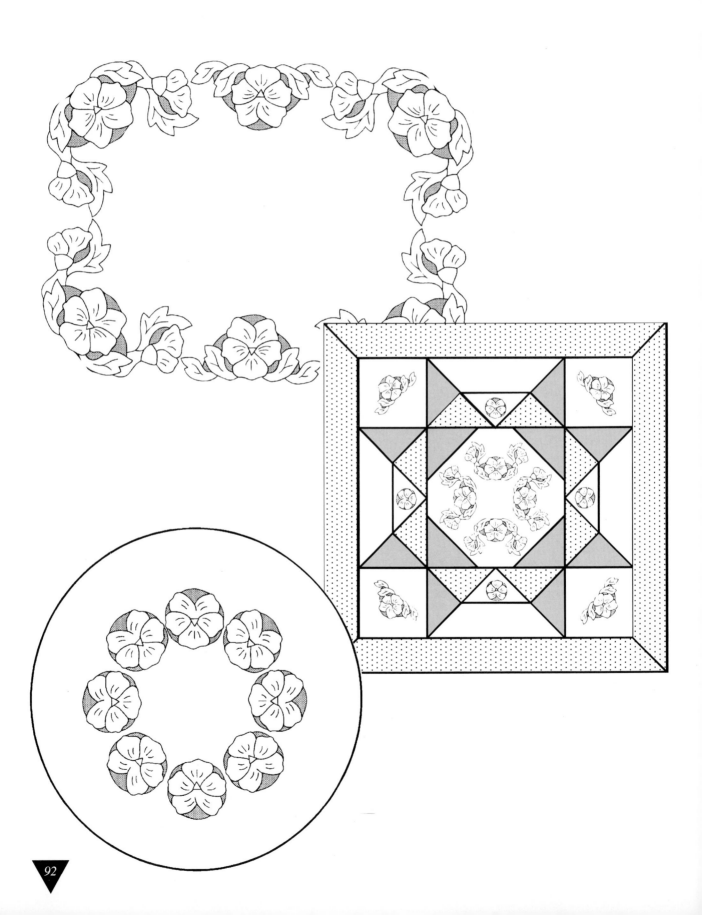

Pansy Design Ideas

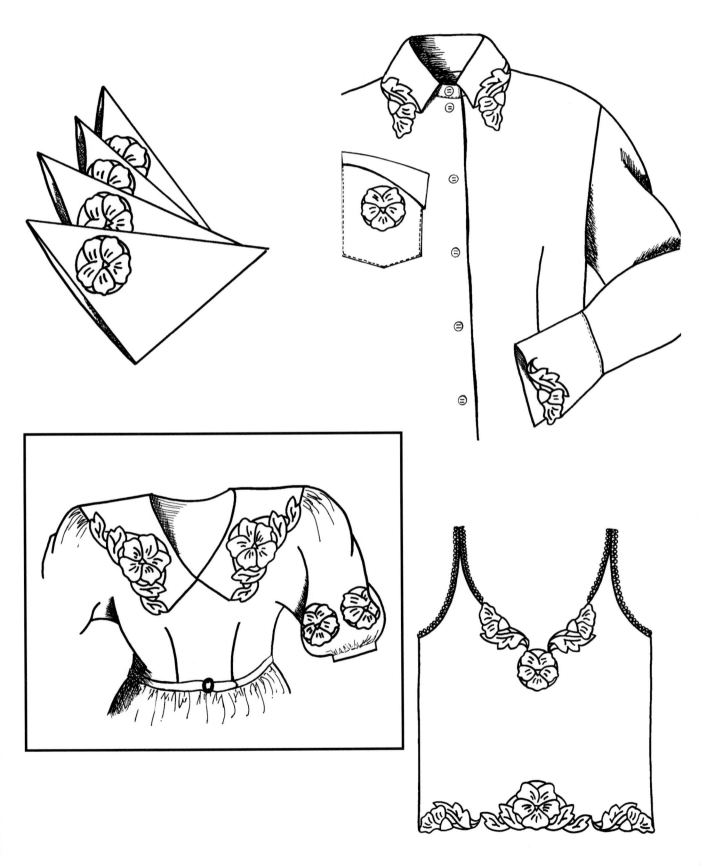

Pansy Section A

NOTE; Sections A,B,C, suitable for edge cutwork

Section C unsuitable for edge

☐ *CUTWORK AREAS*

Pansy Section B

☐ *CUTWORK AREAS*

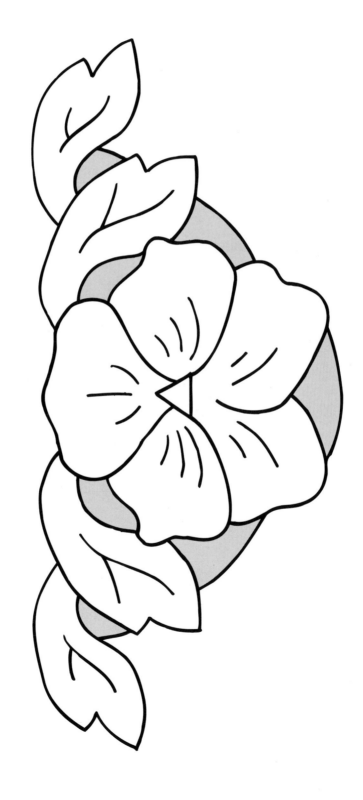

Pansy Section C

□ *CUTWORK AREAS*

Pansy Section D
Left and Right

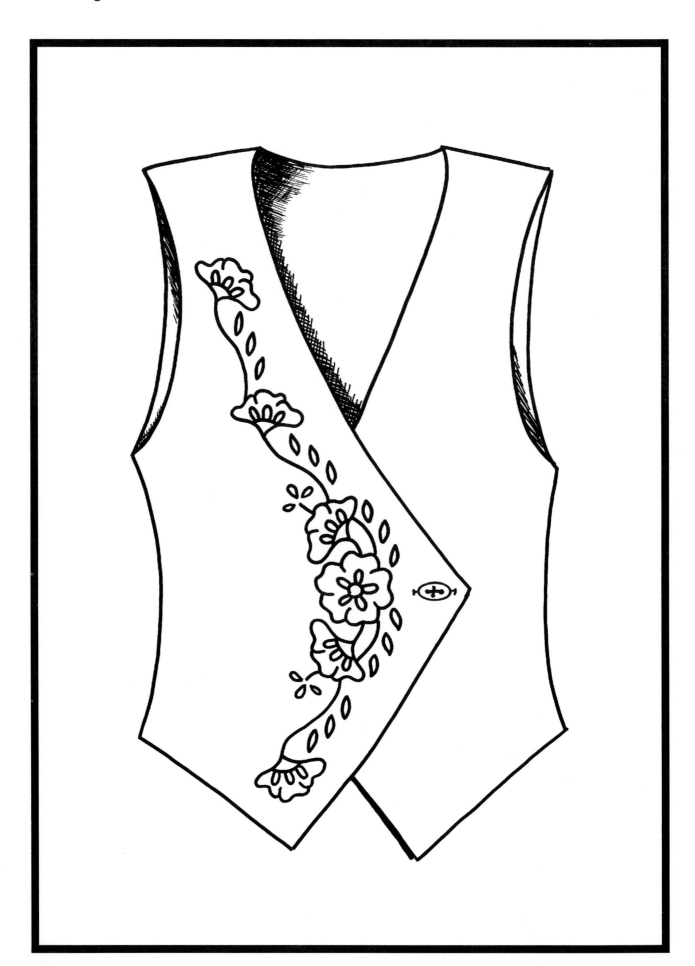

The Rock Rose

This design is inspired by the rock rose that tumbles down the slope at my front door, I love it! Botanically a pink or white flower, I think nature will forgive us if we stitch it in whatever colour takes our fancy.

Stitched using the coloured cutwork technique as shown in chapter 5 brings any design to life. The donna cover on page 22 which is stitched in blues and yellows adds that country touch to the design. Stitched in white it would have a even more traditional look. Any of the seven designs can be stitched using coloured threads, this again opens up the opportunity for you to add your own special touch to your creation.

Design Ideas The Rock Rose

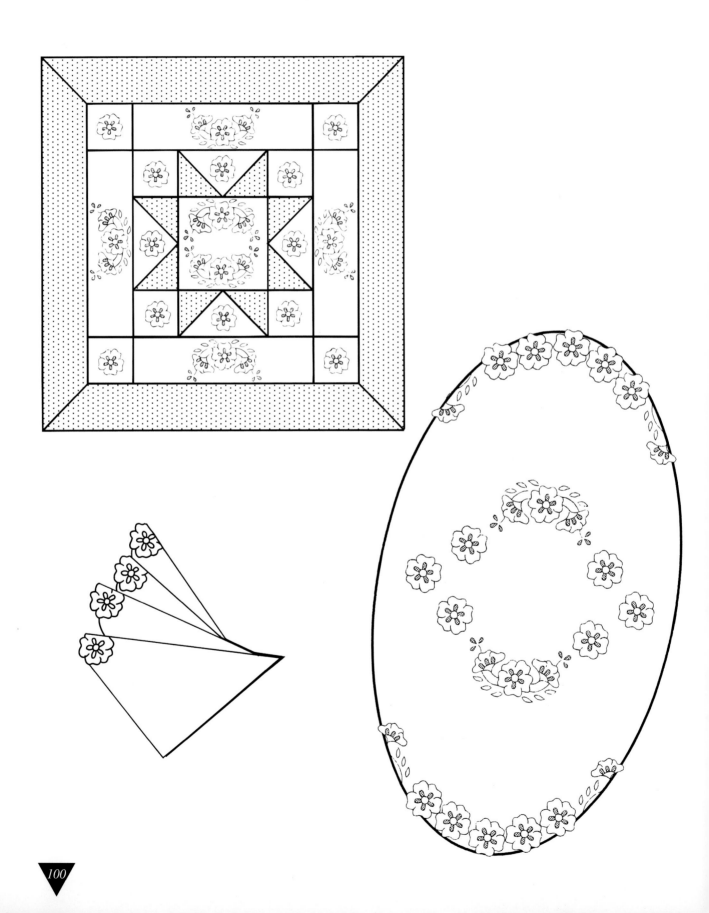

The Rock Rose Design Ideas

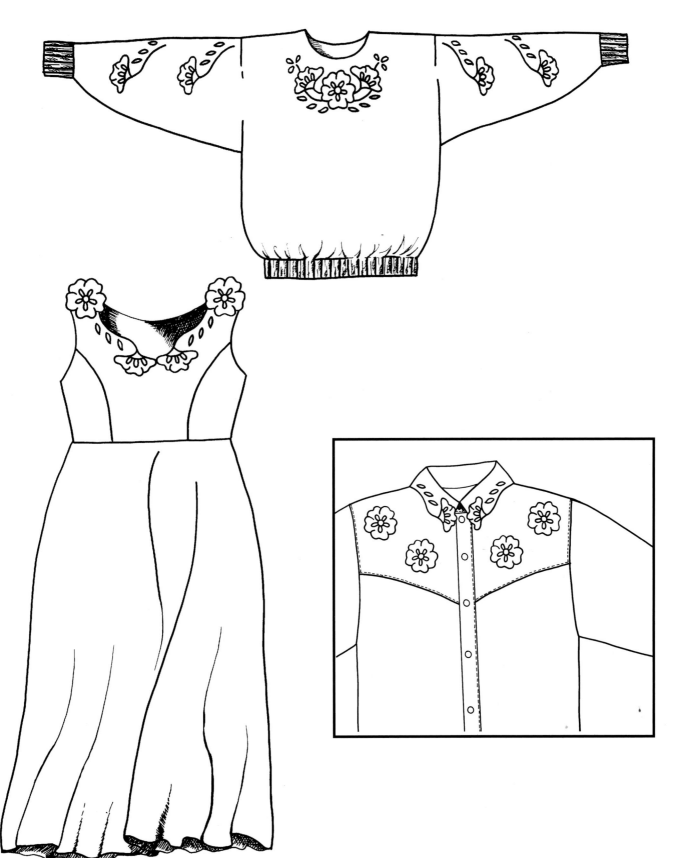

Rock Rose Section A

NOTE; Section B, C suitable for edge cutwork

Sections A unsuitable for edge cutwork

CUTWORK AREAS

Rock Rose Section B

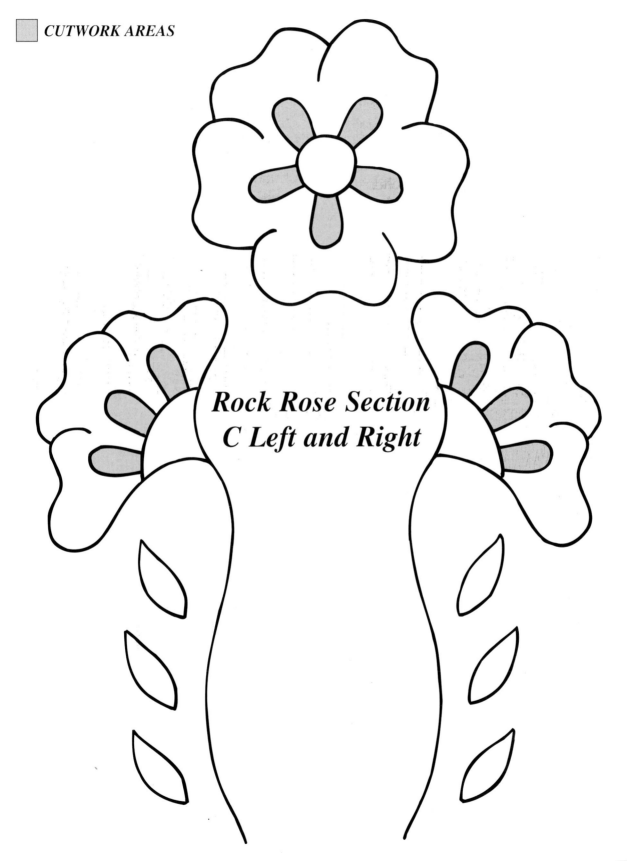

☐ *CUTWORK AREAS*

*Rock Rose Section
C Left and Right*

LOTUS

I created the lotus design so you can go crazy with Richelieu bars, having lots of cutwork areas the lotus is ideal for this simple and fun technique.

Richelieu bars appear as if they would be difficult to stitch by machine, let me assure you they are very simple. You will find the technique instructions in chapter 8 and a cushion stitched with gold Richelieu bars on page 69. I think because we expect the finished effect to be hard to achieve, which it isn't, adds to the fun and thrill of creating them. Richelieu bars can be added to any of the seven designs for that extra special touch.

Design Ideas Lotus

Lotus Design Ideas

Lotus Section A Left

NOTE; Section D suitable for edge cutwork

Sections A,B,C, unsuitable for edge cutwork

CUTWORK AREAS

Lotus Section A Right

 CUTWORK AREAS

Lotus Section B

CUTWORK AREAS

Lotus Section C
Left and Right

Lotus Section D

Notes & Sketches ▼

Mock Orange

Feminine and graceful, you will find the fluid lines of this design a pleasure to stitch.

The quilt on page 9 shows you the true beauty of this design. Any of the seven designs can be incorporated into quite making. If you are after something a little different which will be much admirered, be adventurous and cutwork a quilt.

Design Ideas Mock Orange

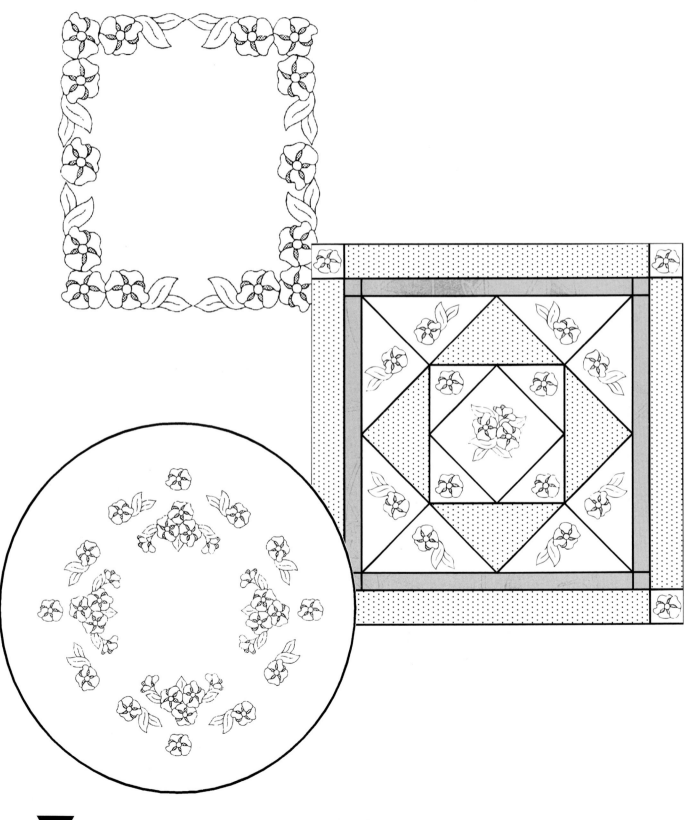

Mock Orange Design Ideas

Mock Orange Section A

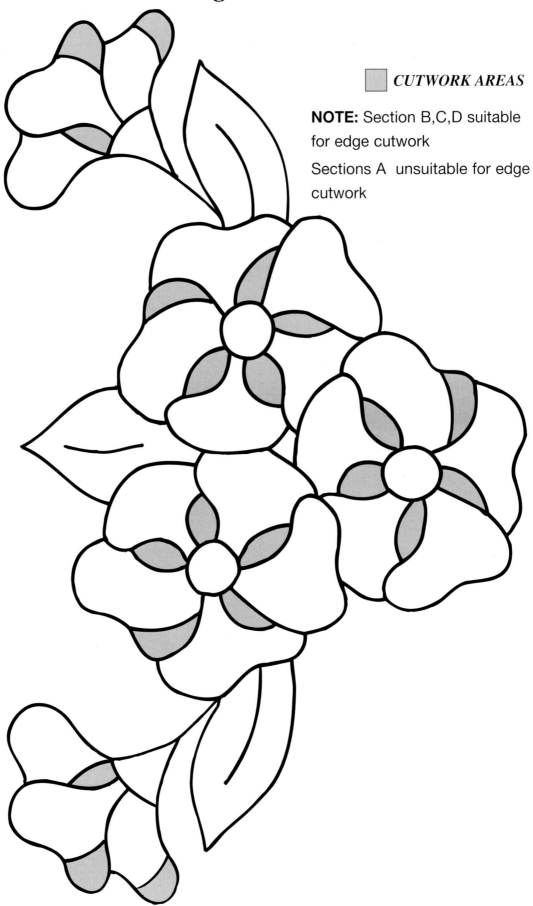

CUTWORK AREAS

NOTE: Section B,C,D suitable for edge cutwork

Sections A unsuitable for edge cutwork

Mock Orange Section B

□ *CUTWORK AREAS*

Mock Orange Section C
Left and Right

▢ **CUTWORK AREAS**

*Mock Orange
Section D*

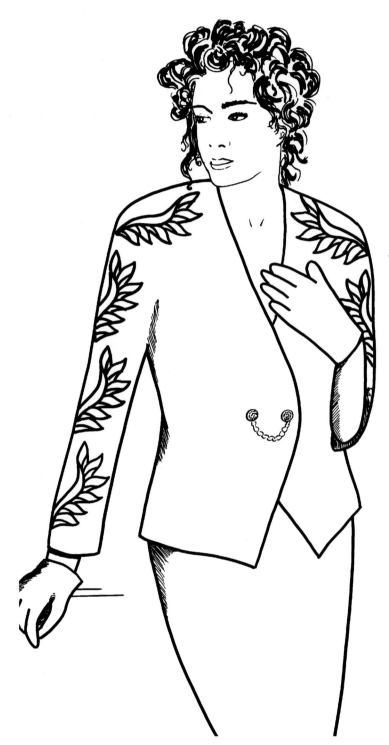

Lyrebird

Being a bird watcher I could not help but draw inspiration from my fine feathered friend the Lyrebird

For those of you outside of Australia the Superb Lyrebird is just that, superb. With tail feathers of over half a meter and a voice that mimics the sounds of its bushland home it is a very special feathered friend.

For a modern dramatic finish stitch this design in strong bold colours. Have a look at the jacket photographed on pages 10-11 and see how cutwork can dramatically break away from the traditional soft pastels.

Design Ideas Lyrebird

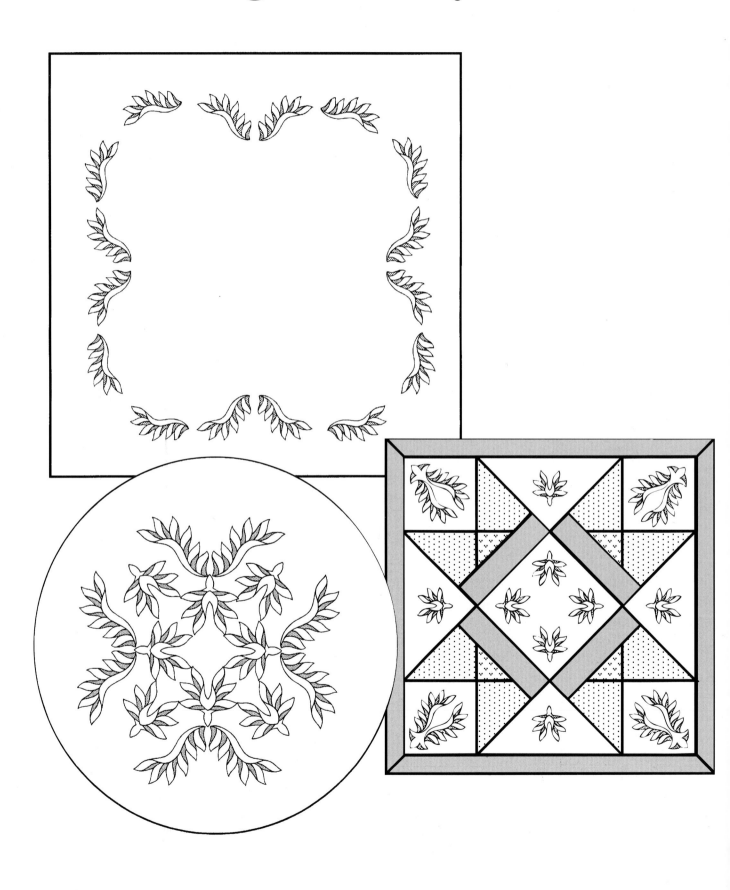

Lyrebird Design Ideas

Lyrebird Section A

NOTE: Unsuitable for edge cutwork

☐ *CUTWORK AREAS*

Lyrebird Section B

☐ *CUTWORK AREAS*

Lyrebird Section C
Left and Right

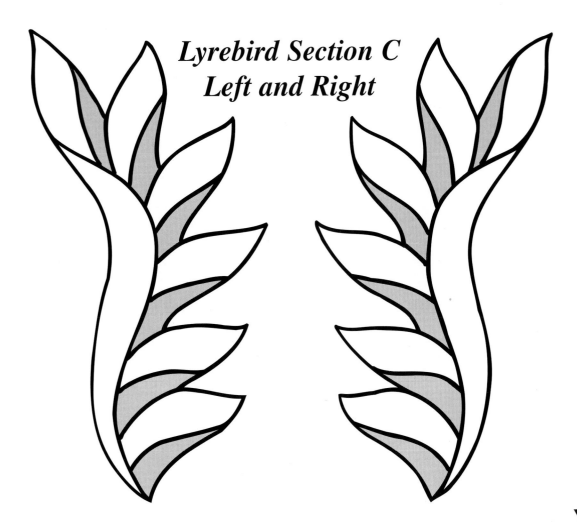

▼ Notes & Sketches

Cutwork Products and Supplies

THE PRODUCTS USED BY MICHELLE FOR

"AN INTRODUCTION TO MACHINE CUTWORK"

AND MANY OTHER EMBROIDERY PRODUCTS

ARE BY M.V. DESIGNS AUSTRALIA AND ARE AVAILABLE

THROUGH GOOD SEWING MACHINE AND FABRIC STORES.

WHOLESALE ENQUIRES WELCOME.

FOR CUSTOMERS WITHOUT A STORE IN THEIR AREA

YOU MAY PURCHASE THESE PRODUCTS

THROUGH THE M.V. DESIGNS MAIL ORDER

CATALOGUE SERVICE.

TO OBTAIN YOUR COLOUR MAIL ORDER CATALOGUE

PLEASE WRITE TO THE ADDRESS BELOW.

M.V. DESIGNS AUSTRALIA

P.O. BOX 841 BEGA NSW 2550.

PH: 064 927211 FAX: 064 927214

▼ Notes & Sketches